BUILDING THE MAINE GUIDE CANOE

JERRY STELMOK

BUILDING THE MAINE GUIDE CANOE

INTERNATIONAL MARINE PUBLISHING COMPANY
CAMDEN, MAINE

Copyright ©1980
by International Marine Publishing Company
Library of Congress Catalog Card Number 80-80780
International Standard Book Number 0-87742-120-X
Typeset by A & B Typesetters, Inc., Concord, New Hampshire
Printed and bound by The Alpine Press, South Braintree, Massachusetts
Drawings by the author.
Third printing

Published by International Marine Publishing Company
21 Elm Street, Camden, Maine 04843

Contents

Foreword

A canoe must fill many unusual requirements: it must be light and portable, yet strong and seaworthy, and it must embody practical qualities for paddle, pole, and sail. It must reject every superfluity of design and construction, yet satisfy the tastes of its owner and safely carry heavy dunnage through unpredictable conditions. These demands will be met by a builder both meticulous and clever—one who, through resourcefulness and dedicated craftsmanship, can build a canoe that will be an everlasting source of joy. It will provide pleasures that continue throughout the four seasons; loving labors that extend from spring refit through a summer and autumn of hard work and play, and on through the winter layup period of redesigning, building, and improving the canoe and its auxiliary gear.

I hope the author's text as well as the experiences of the men who appear throughout the book will impart to the discerning reader a proper understanding of the creation of simple, graceful canoes. It is sad that the practical knowledge and technical skill necessary to build them has remained virtually uncommunicated. One can only hope that revealing a part of this information will result in a clearer understanding of the special bond between the traditional canoeist and the wood-canvas canoe. For indeed, a canoe reflects so clearly the spirit of its builder and user that it develops a character more akin to a living thing than to a mere object of possession.

I have little doubt that from these pages will evolve beautiful water creatures that will be strong, long-lasting, and a source of limitless pleasure for the traditional canoeist traveling the wilderness waterways. These craft will become as much a part of our canoe heritage as the remarkable craft passed along to us from the era reverently referred to as the "Golden Age of Canoeing"—an age of intrinsic values, simple joys, and true resourcefulness, a part of which may still be experienced by those who know the value of building, owning, and using a traditional cedar canoe.

Clint Tuttle
Canoe builder and instructor
of wooden boatbuilding

Preface

When the Cosmic Planetwright designed Earth, he had the foresight to provide for all eventualities. Everything he created was designed to serve some function best, and he had the whole of time laid out before him so as not to leave anything out. This is why birds have trees to nest in and lizards have little crevices in rocks in which to hide from the midday sun.

Even man was designed with some reason in mind, although unraveling exactly what it might be defies the attempts of even the wisest philosophers. Whatever the eventual goal, the Planetwright was generous in providing everything necessary for man to while away his time pleasurably while moving toward or at least awaiting this purpose.

Knowing man to be both restless and adventuresome, the Planetwright graced Earth with vast oceans and secluded lakes and crisscrossed the land with winding streams and rivers, all beckoning the traveler to come and explore their unknown bends and reaches beyond. To allow them to do this he provided trees, particularly cedars, which in turn provided wood, which counts among its wonderful properties the ability actually to float upon the water. Man was also provided with a bit of ingenuity, and it didn't take him long to learn to fashion boats—or, more properly, canoes—from these cedars, as the Planetwright had always intended. To man's great surprise, not only did these handsome craft float, but they demonstrated many other remarkable qualities as well. They were resilient, giving generously whenever they contacted an obstacle in the stream, and then springing back to their original shape unbroken. They were fluid, allowing the paddler to feel the current beneath his feet and to react quickly and surely. And they were silent, dampening any thuds caused by a carelessly plied paddle. For hundreds of years such canoes served mankind in work and play like enduring yet graceful workhorses.

But then man became a renegade, and all over the planet he used his cleverness to misuse the natural gifts afforded him. From Earth's bountiful resources he created chemicals and synthetics that contradicted the original purposes of the creation, and in the process he ravaged the natural bounty, displaced his co-inhabitors, and spread pollution across the land. So overconfident has he become in his technology that he has attempted to build his canoes out of materials that do not even float, canoes that must be fitted with special chambers so they will not sink to the very bottom should they become upset.

And in his reckless push forward, man has lost sight of the very reasons for building a canoe in the first place; he has accustomed himself to the noise, discomfort, unmanageability, and ugliness of his own black handiwork, as though these were no inconvenience whatever. Meanwhile, the abandoned or neglected cedar canoes slide into obscurity, cherished by a few tenacious traditionalists who remember their service well and who will not let them be forgotten, knowing full well that somewhere in the unfurling fabric of existence the Cosmic Planetwright will address this terrible injustice, this unnatural manipulation of his purposes.

Acknowledgments

The text of this book is based primarily upon my canoe-building experience over the past several years. During this period I have accrued a lengthy list of individuals who have in different ways contributed to the qualified success of this endeavor. The list includes sawmill operators, bankers, teachers, the White Canoe people, and other friends, without whom the experience and thus indirectly the book would have been impossible. They know who they are, and to them I express my enduring gratitude.

There is also a smaller group of persons who have contributed directly to the production of this text and who should be individually recognized for their contributions. Clint Tuttle, the craftsman who taught me the intricacies of canoe building in the first place, and who could very well have written such a book of his own, provided needed encouragement as well as several of the photographs illustrating the text. He also generously consented to provide an appropriate foreword, reflecting his dedication as an educator as well as his understanding of the craft. Rollin Thurlow, my partner through thick and thin, graciously accommodated this major upheaval in the shop and pitched in helpfully whenever an extra hand was required to illustrate a procedure properly. Long-time friend Phil DesLauriers devoted a major portion of his spring to helping produce the canoe used for the illustrations, as well as to taking a major portion of the photos. Without such a willing and readily available skilled hand, I might still be fumbling away with one hand on the work and the other on the shutter release button. For a truly professional handling of all phases of the formidable darkroom work necessary for the photographic illustrations, Roger Normand deserves special credit. I became certain more than once that his was the only organized and meticulous hand

xi

holding together the oftimes diverse threads of the endeavor. Finally, Lynn Franklin deserves special thanks and acknowledgment for providing many of the passages that appear between the chapters throughout the book, passages that are designed to give the builder a feeling for the heritage he is helping to continue, as well as a glimpse of the rewards he may hope to enjoy. The passages are selected from a superb collection of such first-person accounts that make up Lynn's forthcoming book on the Allagash wilderness—a unique perspective of the region through the eyes of individuals who have spent a good part of their lives living and learning along this famous river system.

BUILDING THE MAINE GUIDE CANOE

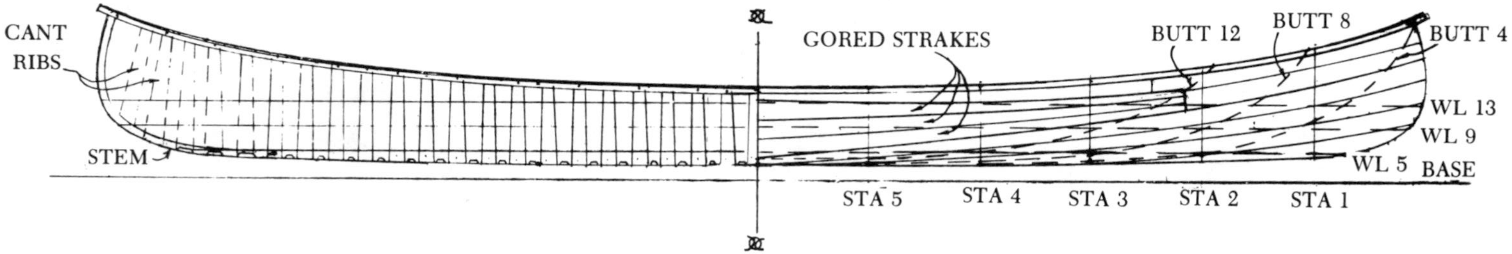

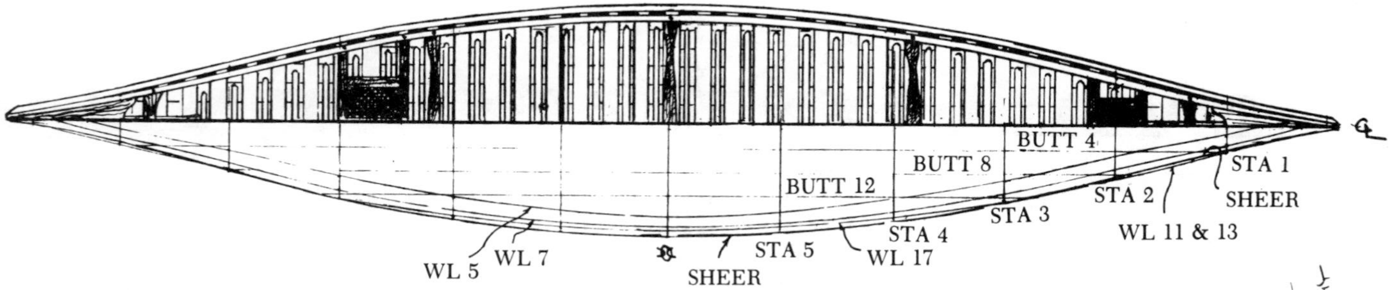

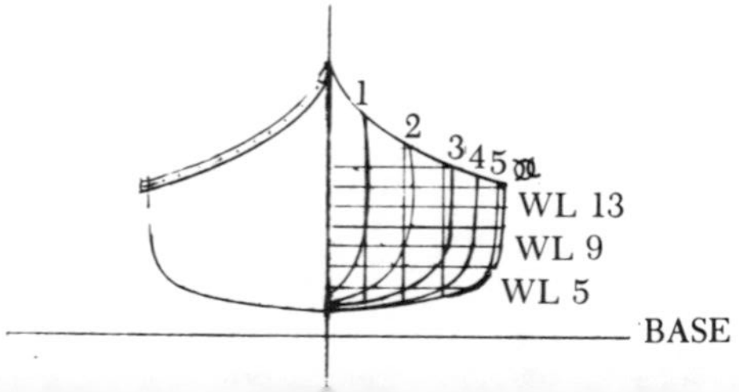

BUTT 4
BUTT 8
BUTT 12
WL 13
WL 9
WL 5 BASE
STA 1
STA 2
STA 3
STA 4
STA 5
GORED STRAKES
CANT RIBS
STEM

STA 1
SHEER
WL 11 & 13
STA 2
BUTT 4
STA 3
BUTT 8
STA 4
WL 17
BUTT 12
STA 5
SHEER
WL 5
WL 7
WL 5
WL 9
WL 13
BASE
1 2 3 4 5

18½-FOOT E.M. WHITE GUIDE CANOE

1

The Wood-Canvas Tradition

Not everyone will buy the admittedly slanted perspective on the creation that was described in the previous pages, and not everyone wants to assume the responsibility of owning a hand-crafted canoe that is bound to require special care and maintenance. Few people who have used wood-canvas canoes and understand them, however, will disagree that they provide an experience that goes beyond simple water transportation.

Contrary to popular belief, building these canoes is not becoming a forgotten art. Throughout the Northeast and eastern Canada, dozens of builders still produce them to meet a steady, if not actually growing, demand, dispelling gloomy prophecies that aluminum and the new plastics would completely eliminate the wood-canvas traditional canoe long before the present. Trite and naive as it sounds, there is something about a wood-canvas canoe that cannot be duplicated by synthetic models. As long as there continue to be free-flowing waters to explore, and people who insist on navigating them in a craft that displays excellent handling qualities as well as beauty and character, there will always be well-designed, well-built wood-canvas canoes—not hung in museums, but on the water demonstrating the qualities that endeared them to so many.

Predecessors of the Wood-Canvas Canoe

The canvas-covered cedar canoe evolved directly from the birch-bark canoes used extensively by the Indians of the Northeast. These bark shells, reinforced with unfastened planking and frames, represent incredible understanding of native materials and remarkable ingenuity in applying a few simple hand tools to a major project. The well-built birch-barks were delightful to perceive, easy to handle, and

1

Canoe party around camp fire, *by Mrs. F.A. Hopkins. (The Public Archives of Canada)*

incredibly resilient. They served nearly all the requirements of the nomadic Indians, who seasonally traveled great distances through otherwise impenetrable wilderness along the myriad watercourses.

Birch-bark canoes did not, however, answer as well the needs of the enterprising white men who began exploring this wilderness with an eye for what might be used to turn a profit; and there was much to be found. The pelts of the furbearers brought handsome prices from European buyers, who converted them into fashionable hats and furs for the chic salons of Paris and London. The colossal stands of virgin white pine beckoned lumbermen, who were to become barons in their own right, acquiring thousands of square miles of land, at first merely for the white pine, which provided unexcelled spars for the British, and later the colonial, navy. Minerals there were, and fish, fowl, and game; and later the wilderness provided urban dwellers a chance to escape the pressures of the grimy industrial cities and refresh their spirits in a remote, primitive frontier.

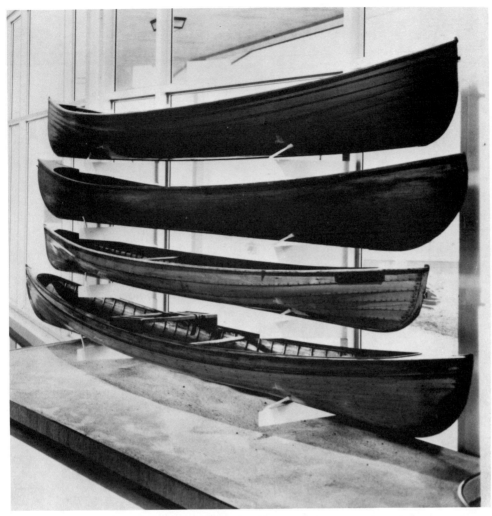

Part of the exhibit, The Adirondack Museum. (Adirondack Museum)

The early trappers and hunters relied heavily on the birch canoes because they were available. Concerned with competition and fluctuating markets, they imposed new stresses on the craft, carrying heavier loads in less time and with less care than the Indians would ever have thought of doing. Still the voyageurs became exceptional canoemen and, next to the Indians themselves, perhaps best understood the principles and limits of the bark canoe. The timber cruisers and market hunters who followed were less tolerant of the bark canoe's shortcomings; because time was synonymous with money, they begrudged any delays that were required to check or mend seams. The recreation-seekers and the guides who served them had their own requirements, and birch-bark canoes became more and more unsuitable, or simply too scarce to keep up with the demands for such a craft.

By the mid-nineteenth century, builders were already addressing this problem in a variety of ways. In New York and Pennsylvania, superb craftsmen began producing lapstrake and bevel-lapped wooden canoes and guideboats, which have never been surpassed for pure beauty and craftsmanship. J. H. Rushton is perhaps the most famous of these builders, whose boats stole the hearts of the burgeoning recreation-minded public through the turn of the century. Sadly, the uncovered canoes were built too well for many enthusiasts. Sales dwindled as prices rose to accommodate increased operating expenses, even though the canoes represented an excellent value to the end. In addition, the canoes were designed to be used by skilled canoeists and were never designed to tolerate the abuses wrought upon them by ignorant owners.

Early Wood-Canvas Canoes

In Maine and eastern Canada the problem was tackled differently, and the wood-canvas canoe was born. Unlike its birch-bark predecessors, the canvas-covered canoe had planking and ribs that were actually fastened with metal tacks, and the hull was built over an improved form that encouraged mass production by eliminating the time-consuming setting-up steps associated with conventional small-boat construction. The one-piece canvas covering was applied after the hull was built, eliminating the nuisance of dealing with underwater seams.

The canoes became instantly popular, and Maine led the way in developing them, probably because of a combination of circumstances: availability of good lumber; a good market in terms of hunters, trappers, and recreation-seekers; and a supply of skilled builders whose ancestors had practiced birch-bark canoe building for generations. E. M. White, Morris, and Old Town were three early leaders in the production of the wood-canvas canoe. Other major builders to follow included Templeton, Skowhegan, and Kennebec. Among them they built thousands of canoes that were shipped throughout the world. Wood-canvas canoes became the preferred work canoes of guides, timbermen, wardens, and rangers, who used them almost daily from ice-out to freeze-up, as well as the pleasure boats of vacationers, who used them for but a month at the cottage in the summer, then stored them in the boathouse. They filled the liveries of summer camps, where thousands of people got their first introduction to the pleasures and rigors of canoeing. Their dominance did not dwindle until after World War II, when people first began getting excited about new marine applications of aluminum, and later, plastics.

With good cedar and spruce becoming scarce, and labor getting more expensive, it didn't take long for the synthetic fabrications to undersell their wooden counterparts. Exaggerated claims about the durability of synthetics and inflated accounts of the maintenance required by the wooden canoes did their part to breed skepticism toward the old reliable wooden canoe.

One by one the factories closed down or converted to plastic fabrication. A few manufacturers continued wooden production, but on a greatly reduced scale. Many forms were destroyed or hauled away by workers, who stored them in their barns and cellars, where they either sat idle or were used to build an occasional canoe at the request of a friend or relative. Some provided a source of extra income for their new owners during the off season.

No. East Carry, Me., Canoe Wagon
loaded for West Branch of Penobscot.

The Wood-Canvas Canoe Today

The situation is much the same today. Nestled throughout Maine are many interesting little shops that turn out a limited number of a particular model of canoe that once was manufactured commercially. The shops vary considerably in sophistication, from sparsely equipped one-man operations in garages to Old Town's relatively modern facility beneath its immense plastic fabrication factory. The canoes themselves also vary considerably, as do ideas about what constitutes a good design.

The builders are an unlikely assortment of individuals, but all share a love of wooden canoes and a dedication to their preservation. Many cover the hulls with fiberglass instead of canvas, claiming it is tougher and more resistant to abrasion, while their opponents insist that canvas is quieter and allows the wood to flex more naturally. Both claim their particular covering is easier to patch in the field, and no amount of debate or information is likely to change the minds of advocates of either method. I prefer the canvas, and that is the method of hull covering discussed in this book. Readers can find plenty of publications dealing with applying plastics to wood, and any builder who feels he would rather fiberglass his hull can get thorough instructions from a number of these sources.

Stop and Think

"Stop and think. You take that canoe and there's no place in the State of Maine you can't go with a pole, a paddle and of course on a big lake you can put a motor on it if you want to. You get a stream that's too shallow to paddle and you got to pole. We used to pole day in and day out. We used to put in on Cross Carry Brook, go up head of the lake on the steamer. Pole all day and into the second day and go to Bog Dam, carry across, snub down the branch. You couldn't do that with anything but a canoe, not travel like that. Fellow down here at the sports shop, he's always trying to sell me a boat, one of them big motors to take on a lake. 'I got just what you want, here,' he says. I says to him, 'You ain't got anything that I want. I can go anywhere that I want to go, and if I got that boat I'd have to yard it somewhere in a lake and I wouldn't be able to get anywhere. If I want to go to Fort Kent, I can go with this canoe.' "

Myron Smart
in an interview with Lynn Franklin

2

Canoe Building in Maine

Vast and unpredictable, Moosehead Lake dominates north central Maine and for many residents and vacationers alike represents the gateway to the North Woods. Pocked with fir-clad islands and penetrated by a hundred peninsulas, the deep, cold lake provides ideal habitat for landlocked salmon and lake and brook trout. In years past, grand hotels and lodges in the region provided the required luxuries for hundreds of wealthy visitors who journeyed to the area by rail to indulge in the outdoor activities provided by the lake and the surrounding wilderness.

The mighty Kennebec River empties from two separate rents in the western shore of Moosehead, and a few miles farther north on the same shore, as though to compensate, the Moose River adds its flow to the lake beneath the shadow of Mount Kineo. North East Carry at the northern tip of the lake is a three-mile portage to the West Branch of the Penobscot, a tributary of Chesuncook Lake, from whence a voyageur may make his way into the Allagash and eventually the St. John system, or, like Henry David Thoreau more than a century ago, follow the arduous, portage-strewn route down Webster Stream into Grand Lake Matagamon, the Penobscot, eventually Old Town, and if desired, Bangor and Penobscot Bay beyond.

Moosehead Region Builders

Understandably, canoes and canoe building have been an important part of the history and economy of the Moosehead region for a long time. At one point at least a dozen builders set up shop along the shores of the lake, most of them around the two logging towns of Greenville and Rockwood. Fred and Arthur Templeton were two of the finest. Although they were cousins, they worked independently—Fred at Greenville and Arthur at Rockwood. Fred Templeton built a 20-foot form in

8

Fred Reckards with two completed canoes, 15-foot and 20-foot Templetons.

1936 and a 15-foot one in 1940. The 20-foot model is a big working guide's canoe, 41½ inches in beam, displaying considerable tumblehome and, although it is only 12 inches deep, boasting a tremendous carrying capacity. After Fred Templeton died, the forms went to Merton Comstock, and the 20-foot model is still referred to by some as the Comstock canoe.

Today the Fred Templeton designs are in the capable hands of Comstock's son-in-law, Fred Reckards, who operates nearly full time in a small shop nestled pleasantly along a fine stretch of the Moose River just outside of Rockwood.

With sparkling eyes and a ready grin, Fred will willingly explain the history of his canoes and the intricacies of the art he practices—if you aren't too pushy, and if

Harold ("Doc") Blanchard builds few canoes to sell nowadays, but he is passing on his knowledge of the art at a successful adult education program.

he should happen to like the looks of you. On the other hand, should you abruptly stomp into his shop, pull out your wallet, and insult his profession and his dedication by offering to buy one of his forms for a few thousand dollars in cash, as one fellow did, you will quickly be shown the exit and asked not to return.

Fred uses finest-grade cedar and spruce and ash in his canoes, and he experiences the same difficulties procuring such lumber as everyone else does. Most of the canoes he covers with fiberglass, leaving a large percentage of them clear, and his work with fiberglass is definitely outstanding. The 20-foot design is the more popular, but the 15-foot one is a nifty little fishing model, very broad of beam and undoubtedly stable enough for comfortable fly fishing. Fred grimaces at the thought of a keel, and indeed most of the fishermen and rivermen who buy his canoes would have little use for one.

Adapting to the chronic shortages of suitable materials, Fred Reckards is increasingly acquiring his wood in the natural round form from local loggers, roughing out stock with his chain saw and then milling the wood into the finished canoe stock. This kind of independence is common to many of his colleagues, and it is this self-reliance that allows men like Fred to continue working at a profession many had considered dead years ago.

Harold ("Doc") Blanchard has built several hundred canoes in the past 25 years or so, all the while working full time as a biologist for the Maine State Fish and

Wildlife Department. Doc lives in Greenville on the southern end of the lake and occasionally builds canoes on his 20-foot Arthur Templeton form, as well as 12-foot and 15-foot canoes on forms of his own manufacture. He is a no-nonsense, efficient organizer, traits that become immediately apparent when you visit him at his office on one of the rare days that inclement weather has kept him from getting out into the field. He is probably the fastest builder in the trade today, planking his 20-footer in just eight hours by himself. His organization comes into play in the wintertime, when he takes on 15 novices at the regional adult education program. After 100 hours, he dismisses them with a pretty good understanding of canoe construction, plus 10 completed wooden hulls. He uses his own two smaller forms in what is becoming a highly popular course, since the students get to keep their canoes for the price of the materials, which is roughly $125.

The 20-foot Templetons built by Doc dominated the downriver racing circuits for years before highly specialized V-bottomed racing craft became popular. With their round bottoms and straight, rockerless keels, the canoes make fast, straight-tracking canoes. They are still in demand, even though Doc isn't especially interested at this point in building a lot of canoes. Understandably, he would like to spend some of his spare time out in the field using one of his craft for a change. Doc prefers canvas covering to fiberglass, explaining that the rigid plastic coating is incompatible with the naturally resilient cedar. Currently, with his forms and special equipment on loan to the adult education program, he doesn't have what could properly be termed his own shop, but should the urge move him, it would take very little time for someone with his skill and dexterity to organize the situation and in record time emerge with a well-built, attractive 20-foot Arthur Templeton guide canoe.

Myron Smart

At Milo, about 40 miles southeast of Moosehead, Myron Smart, in his eightieth year, operates a small one-man shop where he builds a large-capacity 20-foot canoe on a form he built years ago with Harry Edgerly. He also builds a 15-foot canoe and a beamy 11-footer that is light enough to carry anywhere. Myron hasn't built canoes for a living all his life, but since his retirement he has built close to 200 of them, both to occupy his time and to bring in a little extra money. Before that, Myron made his living in what was really the Maine North Woods, guiding sports, trapping, and doing field work as a game manager for the state.

As a guide, Myron was rated among the best at a time when guiding was a tough, competitive profession. With Myron as guide the sport could expect safe, comfortable passages, well-built campsites, good fishing, sumptuous meals (likely cooked on an iron stove stashed at a favored site, and served on a checkered tablecloth), and amiable companionship from a true gentleman.

As a trapper and self-taught naturalist, Myron has become one of the most knowledgeable experts on the behavior of beaver and other furbearers found near the water. As a paddler and poler of canoes, Myron is unsurpassed in skill. Decades of daily practice from ice-out to freeze-up have evolved into a style that reaches beyond mere efficiency and approaches a true art form, no less incredible than the movements of a world-class ballet performer or an outstanding professional boxer.

Myron Smart of Milo with one of his large-capacity 20-footers.

So completely is he attuned to every factor affecting his canoe that the two seem to fuse into a single organism—like the anadromous salmon, gracefully yet subconsciously seeking the best passage up the river.

Myron covers his canoes with fiberglass and bevels the edges of his planking, probably the only builder still taking the time to do this. He is more interested in providing a suitable work canoe at a very reasonable price than he is in fine finish work with absolutely flawless materials and the price tag associated with such attention. He is also skilled at paddle making, turning out a very handy model in poplar or ash, and occasionally maple or cherry.

Willis Thomas

A few miles southwest of Milo on the banks of the Piscataquis River, just outside the shiretown of Dover-Foxcroft, Willis Thomas builds and repairs wooden canoes in the shop alongside his house. A baker by trade, Willis retired almost a decade ago and learned canoe building from an old-time guide, Boot Levenseller, then in his

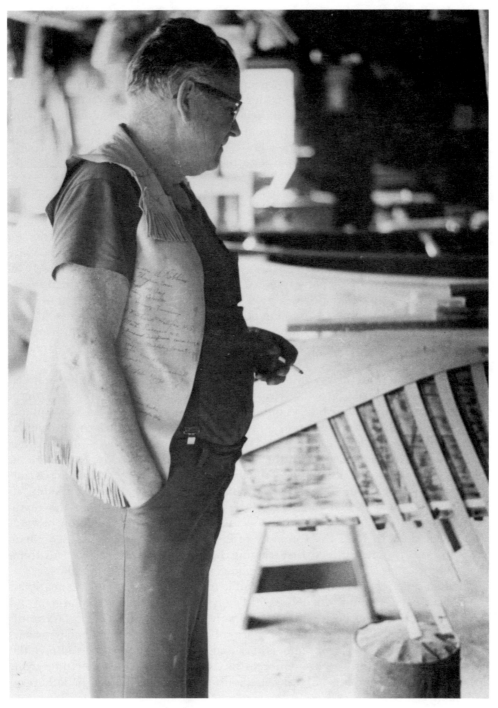

Willis Thomas next to his 12-foot form, with a canoe hull being planked up.

eighties. Eventually, Willis acquired the business, which entails building 12-foot fishing canoes on Levenseller's form and repairing a large number of canoes in various states of disrepair. Until recently, Willis worked alone, but a bothersome leg problem and thoughts of more time afield have prompted him to seek out an apprentice to help with the work and perhaps eventually take over the business. Paul Donnelly, like many of his generation, had tried a variety of things without finding exactly what he was looking for. He feels comfortable in the canoe shop in his native town and has learned a lot from his employer. He looks forward to helping expand the line of canoes to include a few larger models. The Thomas shop covers all the 12-footers with fiberglass and sells them at very reasonable prices, actually competitive with synthetic models.

The Wood-Canvas Canoe Industry

If canoe manufacturing had a cradle, it would have to be the city of Old Town on the Penobscot River just upstream from Bangor. It was here that E. M. White launched the commercial wood-canvas canoe industry in 1889, followed closely by the Old Town Canoe Company founded in 1890 by George A. Gray and incorporated in 1903. Both companies grew to be giants, producing thousands of wooden canoes for shipment throughout the world. White was perhaps best known for its splendidly designed working canoes, and Old Town for its unsurpassed finish, which made Old Town canoes the prized possessions of pleasure canoeists everywhere.

Both companies still thrive, although the town is now dominated by paper mills. White, a medium-sized, growing firm renewed by new ownership after several years of near dormancy, produces only fiberglass models at the Old Town plant. (My partner, Rollin Thurlow, and I build the wood-canvas Whites on the original forms in another town not far distant.) Old Town Canoe Company, on the other hand, has steadily kept pace with the times and grown into the largest nonmetal canoe manufacturer in the nation, producing thousands of synthetic canoes and kayaks in a variety of models and several different plastics. More remarkably, in the lower strata of the immense red brick building, a handful of the many employees still manufacture by hand a much smaller number of the original wooden models. In fact, the company offers a wider variety of wooden canoe models than any other builder, first framing them in native white cedar, sheathing them with western red cedar planking, and covering them with fiberglass.

The two experienced craftsmen responsible for framing and planking nearly all the wooden canoes coming out of the Old Town factory are Emedy Baillargeon and Joe Lavoie. Lavoie has been with the company 15 years, and had 25 years' additional experience with White. He is in charge of the wood canoe shop and is responsible for a large number of innovations and ideas that have streamlined the manufacturing process. He also enforces the strict quality control. Baillargeon, although with the company only 10 years, is unsurpassed as a planker in both speed and quality.

The materials that go into the wooden canoes at Old Town are top quality, although purists criticize the western origin of the Sitka spruce inwales and red

Various completed hulls at Old Town Canoe Company awaiting finishing and covering.

Joe Lavoie of Old Town removes the tape after completing a special-order paint job.

cedar planking. Old Town maintains that it is better able to ensure consistent quality of the materials by procuring such lumber. The canoes are well constructed, and the finish, true to tradition, is painstakingly applied and impeccable. The prices are higher than most, possibly because as part of a larger company, the wooden canoe division has been forced by the accounting department to figure more closely the actual costs of producing a high-quality product—something not always done by the independent craftsman. However you look at it, as long as Old Town Canoe is able to employ dedicated craftsmen like Baillargeon and Lavoie, this long-lived and respected company will continue to produce at least a limited number of fine wooden canoes that will find owners throughout the world.

The Grand Lakers

Changing course and hopping 100 or so miles east northeast, one finds himself in the midst of an impressive chain of lakes, steeped in natural beauty, rich in game fish, and connecting two major rivers in eastern Maine, the Machias and the St. Croix. The Grand Lake chain—Sysladobsis, Junior, West Grand, Big, and East Grand—is the birthplace of a different type of canoe, which has evolved in relatively recent times (since the 1920s) to make safer and more efficient use of the newfangled outboard motor. The Grand Lake Stream canoe has to be one of the most seaworthy craft of its size anywhere. Basically a high-freeboard, beamy canoe with a transom instead of the traditional pointed stern of the double-ender, the Grand Laker satisfies the special requirements of guides faced with the problem of safely and quickly transporting sports around these large, fickle lakes in search of fish.

Among the distinguished developers of this style of canoe were Herb Bacon and Joe and Bill Sprague, each putting into his design the special features he considered most critical from his own considerable experience. The results were gratifying, and the square-sterned canoes became respected wherever large, open bodies of water were found. The Grand Lakers are definitely specialized craft, and no one would want to tote one into a distant beaver pond for trout fishing—the average one weighs in at around 160 pounds. Likewise, poling one up the West Branch during low water would be a futile endeavor at best, because of the poor maneuverability resulting from the long, straight bottom and the constantly snagging keel. However, should you happen to be out in the middle of a large northern lake when an unexpected blow lashes the surface into a frothing, churning maelstrom, and your one desire is to get ashore as quickly, safely, and relatively dryly as possible, the Grand Lake Stream canoe would serve you very well.

In late September, the mixed forest lining both sides of the road into Grand Lake Stream from U.S. Route 1 is a brilliant patchwork collage in gold, orange, and dark green. At the tiny village a bridge spans Grand Lake Stream itself just above the tin-roofed rearing pools of the state fish hatchery. The bridge leads to a launching ramp near the small dam that regulates the water level of lake and stream alike. At the base of the dam in the clear water, the shadowy forms of a dozen or more landlocked salmon hold motionless before the screens of the spillways within the no-fishing zone.

In one of the several boathouses that reach out into the cove in the vicinity, a capable-looking gentleman is putting the finishing touches on a handsome 20-foot Grand Laker, just hours before the eager owners, who have waited a couple of years for their canoe, will be driving up to take delivery. Laurence ("Pop") Moore looks more like a Maine guide than the ones depicted on all the old barbershop calendars. Having grown up in the region, Pop built his first canoe as a teenager under the tutorship of Joe Sprague. Upon retirement, Sprague passed his form on to Pop, who has been building canoes on it ever since.

That was in 1938. Now, when he is not building a hunting or fishing lodge on some remote corner of the lake (employing an authentic coastal lobster boat that barely fits into the covered bay of the boathouse for transporting materials) or guiding an occasional fisherman, Pop can be found at one of his shops building a 19- or 20-foot Grand Laker on the old form. The boats are deep and wide, carrying their beam almost to the wide transom, accommodating safely an outboard motor up to 10 h.p. Because he is a friend of many loggers in the heavily forested region, Pop has managed to secure some of the finest long-length white cedar imaginable, which he puts to excellent use planking the rugged canoes. The ribs are a full ⅜ inch thick and the transom is cut from solid mahogany. The planking is long and clear, and the rails are one-piece clear spruce.

Since Grand Lakers are normally trailered and are too heavily built to pull gently up a rocky beach, Pop covers the hulls with fiberglass. He installs a heavy ash keel and a handsome external ash stem. The canoes look like capable rowing boats as well as gasoline-powered vessels.

Pop does not like being pressured and will not take a deposit with an order, because he feels it might later interfere with his independence in case he should decide to alter his loose production schedule. He builds the hulls in a small, cluttered shop next to his house, a mile or two out of town. The shop contains the well-used form and the few pieces of vintage equipment. Pop then transfers operations to his boathouse at the dam for finishing. The finished product is beautiful, capable, and well worth the reasonable price, even if you do have to wait two years to get it.

Jon Capozza

Jon Capozza operates the Androscoggin Boat and Canoe Company in Wayne, Maine, a hoot and a holler from both Androscoggin Lake in Wayne and the Belgrade Lake chain outside Augusta. Jon is a well-educated, energetic young individual who accomplishes what he sets out to do. What he has done is set himself up in a neat little shop, where he rebuilds canoes and meticulously restores vintage Chris-Craft powerboats. He also builds canoes to order, and, like everything else, he does it well. Currently Jon has an old form for an 18-foot Skowhegan guide canoe as well as two he built himself—one for a 14′9″ double-ended Rangeley boat and another for a wood-canvas version of Rushton's Nomad sailing canoe. Disdaining work with the noxious fiberglass, Jon covers his canoes with canvas only—or you can purchase a hull from him and glass it yourself.

Despite his youth, Jon holds a master's degree and was involved in a number of business enterprises and administrative positions before turning to his new profession, which he finds much more fulfilling and generally more enjoyable. He also attended the boatbuilding program at the vocational school in Lubec, Maine, a few years back and served a distinguished and (we hope) rewarding apprenticeship at our canoe shop, the Island Falls Canoe Company, in preparation for his current enterprise. The Skowhegan model now built by Jon was a popular, manageable craft in the heyday of canoeing, originally manufactured in the Kennebec Valley town by that name.

The Island Falls Canoe Company

Finally, I will briefly mention the Island Falls Canoe Company, located in Atkinson, Maine. It is owned by Rollin Thurlow, a young Maine Maritime Academy graduate, and me—sole authorized builders of the original E. M. White wood-canvas canoes. Since readers will have plenty of opportunity to acquaint themselves with our shop and work in the text of the book, I will add only that in addition to the 18′ 6″ guide model built for illustrating the text of this book, we also build 14-, 16-, and 20-foot White canoes to special order and rebuild old canoes as well.

This is but a partial listing of the builders currently active in Maine, but it does provide a brief survey of the state of the art of wooden canoe building in this region, as well as a glimpse of this strange fraternity of independent souls dedicated to the preservation and promotion of what we all feel is the ultimate versatile craft for North American waters.

The New Canoe

As I pulled her off the carrying racks, I wondered what name I should call her by. This was to be her maiden voyage, and I was eager to test her character, appraise her potentialities.

Mona, Charity, and I had driven over to Old Town the previous day to pick her up at the factory. She had been built to order: no keel, extra half-ribs, very light planking, and a thin coat of hard enamel instead of the heavier lead-containing paint. The ladies had avowed she was pretty, quickly adding that she was, in fact, altogether too lovely and fragile a thing to submit to the savage attack of rock-filled rivers. I agreed she was beautiful but insisted she must have some character as well. She had a mission in life. Hers not to dally amongst preening swans on a placid lily pond; hers to run the rapids, the foaming white waters, the knife edged boulders, despite her tender frailty.

I slid her into the river where she rode pert and high, like a teal. She responded quickly to the paddle and obviously was happy to be in her proper element. We negotiated the first set of rapids. She shuddered at the first painful contact with a jagged rock, but regained composure and settled down to business with the proper spirit and determination. I guessed we would get along together and maybe someday she would develop that dauntless imperturbability that her predecessors had had. Time would tell.

Dale Rex Coman
Pleasant River

3

Canoe Forms

The wood-canvas canoe might never have risen to the height of popularity it once attained had it not lent itself to production over the solid building form. This development allowed the builder to produce a canoe hull as fast as he could rib it out and plank it up, without the time-consuming steps of setting up the molds and attaching the ribbands each time, as required with the construction of most small wooden boats.

The traditional canoe forms of the large manufacturers were so well built that many of them are still either in service or at least in serviceable condition today. The E. M. White forms we are fortunate enough to have in our shop have been used to build literally thousands of canoes, and the Old Town Canoe Company is likewise still using some of its original forms. Most of the small-scale builders scattered throughout our region produce their hulls on vintage forms obtained from some manufacturer or other.

The construction of such a form is no light undertaking; it is more complicated than building the canoe itself. The economics of the project in terms of both capital investment and time are justified only by the continued production of canoes on the form once it is built. Although building a canoe form is a gratifying and interesting project, it cannot be considered a cost-beneficial enterprise for someone interested in building himself a canoe or two. It is, however, a very worthwhile project for a canoe club or outdoors organization that would be able to pool time and resources in the construction of the form, and then benefit from the project by having several canoes built by and for the members. It is an ideal way to exercise woodworking skills and end up with a superbly useful piece of work.

The Molds

The basis for the form is a number of stations or molds, which provide the shape of the hull at various intervals along the backbone. The molds represent exact cross

22

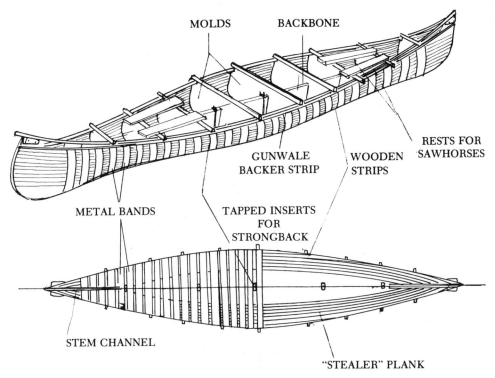

MOLDS   BACKBONE

RESTS FOR
SAWHORSES

GUNWALE
BACKER STRIP

WOODEN
STRIPS

METAL BANDS

TAPPED INSERTS
FOR
STRONGBACK

STEM CHANNEL

"STEALER" PLANK

Parts of the canoe form.

With this method of taking off lines, tacks are carefully laid along the desired station on the full-size body plan so that the edges of the heads leave an imprint of their shape in the plywood.

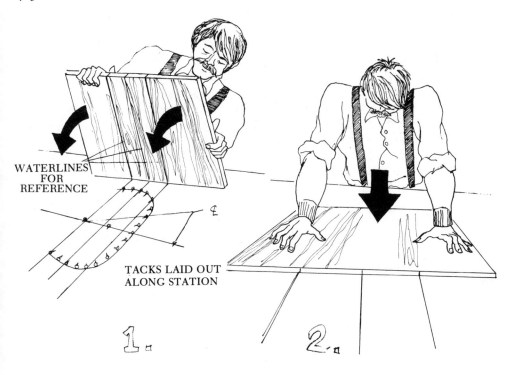

WATERLINES
FOR
REFERENCE

TACKS LAID OUT
ALONG STATION

1.

2.

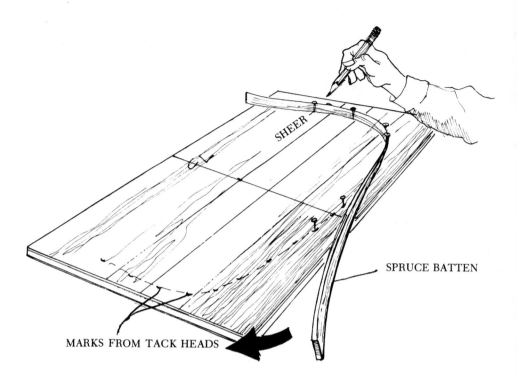

The imprints of the nail heads (see page 23) are connected with a spruce batten, the curve is drawn and cut out on the bandsaw.

sections of the interior of the canoe at specified points along the hull, and they are secured to a backbone piece in such a manner that the waterlines (horizontal cross sections through the length of the hull) are in perfect alignment with one another from mold to mold. The shape of each mold is taken from the body plan on the mold loft floor, as shown in the figure, or may be taken directly by spiling the shape of an existing canoe from the inside surface. (Several books discuss the procedures of taking off lines, lofting, and mold construction much more comprehensively than can be dealt with here.) The actual size of the molds built from such patterns must take into account the thickness of the wooden strips that will sheathe the form, as well as the rib and planking thicknesses if the dimensions are to represent the interior of the canoe accurately.

The molds may be solid ¾-inch plywood, or they may be constructed from spruce stock held together with plywood gussets and internal braces. The molds are notched at the sheer line to provide for the strips of ash or spruce that run the length of the form and will serve as backers and clamping pieces for the internal gunwales. These strips are commonly ⅞" x 1" and are screwed to each of the stations. They are recessed into the molds enough to ensure that the outside surface of each gunwale is flush with the surface of the form itself.

Spiling the shape of a mold inside a canoe. The half-section is cut roughly to shape to begin the exercise, then it is held plumb in the level canoe with a level.

The ends of the form generally duplicate the shape of the intended canoe, although they do not absolutely have to. The stems are prebent over a separate jig, and the planking is not fastened to the stem until the hull has been removed from the form. If there is some provision on the last mold to tie the ends of the stems into place, the bow shape may be eliminated from the form altogether. Pictures of the J. H. Rushton shop in upstate New York show this type of form, although most Maine-built forms have the ends built into them.

The Sheathing

The ¾-inch or ⅞-inch square strips that sheathe the form may be made from spruce or pine. The stock must be nearly free of knots to produce the best results. The strips are attached to each of the stations with 2-inch ring nails and to each other between the stations with smaller-gauge 1¼-inch ring nails as each strip is attached. A wide, shaped plank the thickness of the strips is used along the backbone to begin the sheathing. It is wide amidships, tapering as it approaches the ends, and is designed to take up much of the variable girth along the canoe, allowing the strips to parallel the sheer line of the canoe more closely at all points. The strips are beveled on the inside surface where they meet the ends of the form. If there are no ends as such, as in Rushton's forms, the strips simply end at the last station.

The first few strips require a great deal of twisting at the ends (nearly 90 degrees

Typical molds. These are made of spruce with plywood reinforcements.

The ends of this form closely resemble the ends of the canoe to be built.

on a flat-bottomed canoe) to get them to lie properly along the stations. This problem diminishes as the strips approach the sheer, where they require almost no twisting. Some beveling is necessary to get the strips to fit tightly against one another along the outside seam, but this is not really essential; the form need not be watertight, merely durable.

The strips should roughly parallel the sheer at the gunwales. An exact duplication is not mandatory because the sheer line is already determined by the gunwales locked into the molds, and the final sheer planking is attached after the canoe has been removed from the form. Grooves are provided at both ends along the backbone to serve as a channel for holding the stems in place. The depth of this channel is determined by the thickness of the stem stock minus the depth of the notch cut into the stem to accommodate the ribs. The ribs must bend fairly over the notches without distorting the profile of the bottom of the canoe.

Fairing

The form must be carefully faired and sanded before the metal bands are attached. Making a template for each of the stations will help ensure the symmetry of the corresponding sections of the form. The templates are used to shape the form exactly

The stem in place in the channel provided for it.

at each of the stations with the intervening surface areas faired accordingly. A spokeshave works well for removing any extra wood. When the surface has been faired with the cutting tools, the final smoothing is achieved by sanding. A long-based fairing block as described in Chapter 5 is a surprisingly efficient device for completing this task, and a final sanding is done by hand with a regular-size sanding block or a flat-based orbital power sander. The importance of achieving fairness at this stage cannot be overemphasized; each canoe built subsequently will reflect any flat spots or distortions in the form itself, and the builder will be forever reminded of his laxness or oversight.

The Metal Bands

The galvanized metal bands may be cut from standard heat ducting or purchased specifically from a sheet metal shop. The edges must be clean and smooth to prevent the ribs from being stained or damaged. A variety of thicknesses will work, although 0.025 is ideal. Bands that are too heavy require many fastenings to hold them in place, and each hole in the galvanized metal has the potential of staining the wood with rust. Metal that is too thin to turn the points of the tacks under is even more troublesome, because the fastenings don't clinch, and the hull is effectively fastened to the form when it comes time to remove it. To be completely effective, the metal should be capable of turning the tacks even when they are unsupported with the wooden strips.

The strips are cut long enough to span the specific girth, thus requiring fastenings (⅞-inch No. 8 screws) at each end and along the centerline only. Frequently, the strips are cut a bit long, and the metal is actually bent around the sheer strip, eliminating the danger that the exposed metal will stain the ribs. Both edges of the metal must be flush with the wood, and in the quarters especially, this will mean that the ends of the strips will actually lean or cant back amidships. Since the steamed wood has this same tendency, it is not a serious problem. The bands must be cut to accommodate the stem channel at each end of the form. The builder should lay out the spacing ahead of time and stick to it as faithfully as possible. The bands should be approximately the width of the rib stock to be used, normally 2¼ or 2⅜ inches.

Occasional treatment with a polyurethane varnish becomes necessary to prevent rust from bleeding into the moist wood from scratches or worn spots in the zinc coating. The varnish must be allowed to dry to its maximum hardness, however, before the form can again be used.

Gunwale Backers

The gunwale backers can now be set into the notches provided for them on each mold along the sheer line. A full-length piece of clear spruce is the best material for achieving a fair curve between molds as well as satisfying the demanding structural requirements. Lacking spruce, the builder will do well with a strip of ash or oak. The piece should be screwed into the molds, and if the sweep at the ends is dramatic, these pieces as well as the actual gunwales of the canoe have to be

The function of the steel bands becomes apparent here. These are still in good shape after being used hundreds of times.

Another way to construct the ends of the form. The strip planking and gunwale backers end at the last mold. (The form is shown suspended overhead for storage purposes.)

The rugged hardwood pieces are ideal for suspending the form from ceiling brackets (above) as well as for setting the form on sawhorses.

steamed and prebent over a jig, as described in a later chapter. The ends of each backer are beveled to fit flush against the ends of the form.

A strip of hardwood the width of the thickness of the molds and about ¾ inch thick is screwed across the top of each mold to enclose the gunwale backer in a three-sided notch. These pieces must be well fastened because they are subjected to considerable pressure when the gunwales are set into place for the actual canoe construction. At each end of the form a small piece of hardwood is installed directly above the backer (when the form is in its upside-down building position) to serve this same function.

Although hooks can be fashioned and attached to the molds for holding the gunwales fast, C-clamps can be just as effective and can be placed more freely along the sheer to accommodate special requirements. On each quarter of the form, two pieces of hardwood stock 1 inch thick, long enough to span two molds, allow the form to be set on horses for construction. These are screwed securely to the hardwood strips that hold the gunwales in place.

Other Preliminary Construction Details

Another addition that makes canoe construction easier is the installation of tapped metal inserts for bolting the strongback onto the form. The strongback (generally a length of 2 x 4 running from stem channel to stem channel) keeps the ribs flush

The metal fitting next to the mold secures the tapped metal insert on the outside of the form, which holds the strongback in place.

against the metal bands along the centerline of the form. Three or five bolts are normally employed to hold this member in place, as the steamed ribs are slid beneath it during the frame-bending process. The ⅜-inch-thick metal pieces are drilled and tapped to accommodate the ⅜-inch bolts and are set into the wood between the metal bands along the centerline. They are held in place by two lengths of ⅜-inch threaded rod that run through the form and are threaded into similar metal pieces that span the backbone inside the form.

The well-built form will serve for the construction of hundreds of canoes. The person who has completed the task of building one has a right to be proud of the accomplishment and can proceed to the actual canoe construction with justifiable confidence and positive anticipation. Solving the problems encountered during such a project has prepared him for the toughest challenges awaiting him in building a canoe. Each of the canoes built on the form will have his mark upon them. If they are functional and distinctive, as well as carefully built, it is conceivable that his own form will be retained and revered even after his time, as with the forms of White, Gray, Templeton, and many other distinguished designers and builders.

To the person interested simply in building a canoe for his own use, all this probably has sounded pretty impractical, and most likely he is unable to locate an existing form to use for such a project. This does not mean that he should give up the idea of building a canoe. The principles of small boat construction can be applied

The form with gunwales clamped in place and the strongback bolted on ready for rib bending.

The inside of a form that is suspended from ceiling brackets. Shown are: backbone, molds, gunwale backer strip, and transverse hardwood strips for holding rails in place.

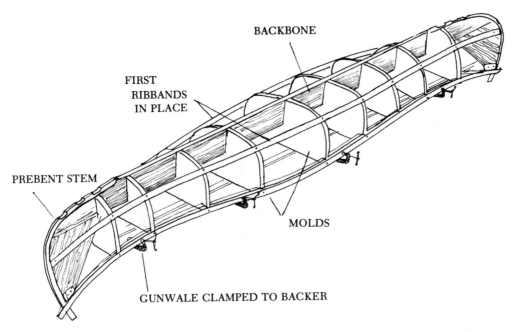

BACKBONE

FIRST
RIBBANDS
IN PLACE

PREBENT STEM

MOLDS

GUNWALE CLAMPED TO BACKER

The initial stages of building a single canoe. The molds have been secured to the backbone, the gunwales and stem are set in place, and the first ribbands are attached on each side.

The remainder of the ribbands have been put in place, the strongback is set and braced, and some of the ribs are bent over it.

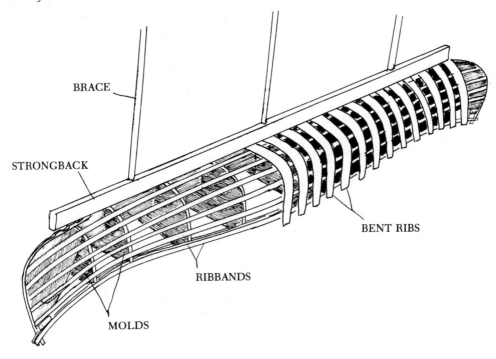

BRACE

STRONGBACK

BENT RIBS

RIBBANDS

MOLDS

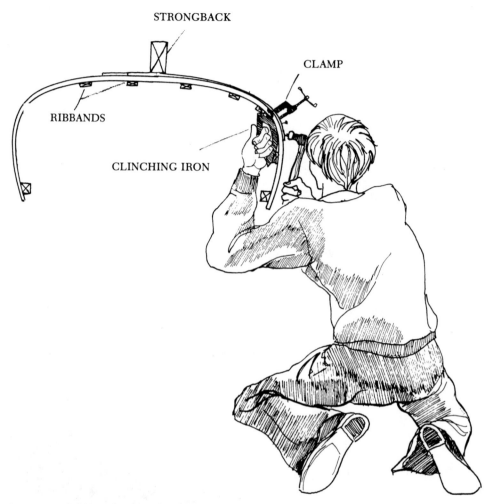

STRONGBACK

CLAMP

RIBBANDS

CLINCHING IRON

The builder will have to clamp the planking strakes in place and back up the tacks with a clinching iron. For hard-to-reach areas of the canoe, a helper is almost a must.

to build a single canoe with excellent results, although naturally with a bit more work than by the form method.

One might proceed as follows:

Begin by making spruce or solid plywood molds exactly as with the solid canoe form. Since the canoe does not have a rabbeted keel, as a conventional boat does, these molds must be mounted onto a backbone piece exactly as in the initial stages of the form construction. Notch the backbone to accommodate the stems.

Lay out six or seven ribbands on each side of the hull along the length of this framework. The spacing of these strips on the various molds is predetermined by mathematically dividing the girth of the particular station by the number of rib-bands to be used. For example, if seven ribbands are to be used on each side of a canoe with a 28-inch half-girth amidships, they would be spaced 3⅔ inches apart after deducting for their combined 1-inch widths. At the end of the canoe, where the half-girth is only 22 inches, the ribbands will be only 2⅓ inches apart. Screw the ribbands directly to the molds and allow them to end at the last station. Provide a gunwale backing strip, just as with the solid form construction. Screw a few small blocks of wood about ⅜ inch thick to the backbone to provide a gap between the form and the strongback through which the ribs can be slid during frame bending. Fasten the strongback to these blocks by counterboring the 2 x 4 and using 3-inch screws. Clamp the inner gunwales and prebent, shaped stems into place before beginning construction. The spacing of the ribs is predetermined and marked on the ribbands.

Then proceed as described in the following text, steaming and bending the frames and planking the hull. The one major disadvantage you will encounter is the absence of the metal bands that clinch the canoe tacks automatically. This means you will have to clamp most of the planking in place and then back up the tacks between ribbands with some type of clinching iron. Along the centerline and in other difficult-to-reach areas, you may require a helper to hold the iron in place. Also, because of the interfering molds and ribbands, some fastenings will have to be skipped until the canoe is removed from the form. Overall, you should be able to clinch enough fastenings to hold the hull together with no major difficulties. As with the conventional form, all but the garboard planks are allowed to run freely by the stem without fastening. When the canoe is removed from the form, follow the procedure outlined in the text to complete the canoe.

The E. M. White

"If you have a picture in your mind of what kind of canoe the Indians made with a big high bow, it's not right. Actually the Indians used to come up from Tobique, had just the same as an E. M. White. The Penobscots also. I always used an E. M. White canoe. It was the original guide canoe, the nearest thing to what the Indians used."

Myron Smart

"He had an E. M. White 20-foot canoe, very safe even with a load. All the Indians from there use White canoes, a few have Skowhegan, not too many. And they have 20-foot because when it gets rough they want to survive it. Live a little longer."

Al Nugent

"The sheer line on the canoe is important. The sheer line on the E. M. White was identical to the Passamaquoddy. They were not swept up in the bow and stern like the Ojibway lake canoes."

Mick Fahey

"I'd like to have had a canoe as good as that one I had back in 1915. First White I ever bought. When I was guiding I had it come up on the Maine Central to Rockwood. It cost me $86 delivered in Rockwood. I run that canoe about 10 years before I had it recanvased. I thought a lot of that canoe, boy. Why, in all the time I guided I only used up four canoes."

Myron Smart

"Yes, sir. The old E. M. White is the guide canoe of Maine and northeastern Canada. The Templeton model is another good canoe—same length and width and quality of craftsmanship. The bottom is a little more round than the White and so the Templeton moves a little easier on the lake."

Mick Fahey

in interviews with Lynn Franklin

4

Materials

In examining the development of the wood-canvas canoe in the Northeast, we have seen that the availability of prime materials played a significant role in this sector's early domination of the industry. The original native woods are still available today in limited quantities to anyone determined enough to seek out the sources, and proven substitutes as good or nearly so as the originals are much more readily available. And since ingenuity played so large a role in the development of the canoe anyway, a little dose of it applied to this problem by the prospective builder might easily unearth some new, yet unappreciated, substitutes with excellent qualities.

Breaking down the canoe into its component parts, let us look at the materials used in the original canoes and discuss some possible substitutes.

Ribs

The frames or ribs are the major structural supports of the hull and perform a truly demanding function. They must be light, strong, and capable of taking severe bends when they are steamed onto the form. They must hold their shape yet display a high degree of flexibility when the canoe is in use. Indeed, the reason such a lightly built craft can withstand such severe stresses, often while heavily loaded, is the natural resilience of its framing materials. Resistance to rot is another important factor, particularly because the vast majority of canoes are used predominantly in fresh water.

Eastern white cedar satisfies all these requirements beautifully, provided the stock is clear of knots and decay. Fortunately, canoe ribs are not particularly long. The longest rib on a typical 20-foot guide canoe, for example, is less than 60 inches in length, and the overall average for most canoes is somewhat less than 48 inches.

40

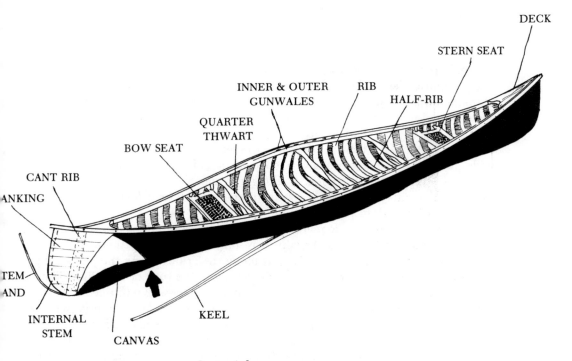

DECK

STERN SEAT

INNER & OUTER
GUNWALES

RIB

HALF-RIB

QUARTER
THWART

BOW SEAT

CANT RIB

ANKING

TEM
AND

INTERNAL
STEM

CANVAS

KEEL

Parts of the canoe.

This makes what would otherwise be an impossible goal attainable, at least for builders in the eastern portion of the country. Short lengths of cedar (4 to 8 feet) in clear grades are often available from shingle mills, manufacturers of fence posts and picket fences, and even commercial builders of log homes—although they are usually in the natural round form, as opposed to the more easily handled square stock with which most of us are accustomed to dealing. Simply obtaining the material is more important than its form at this stage, however, and the builder can always find a way to get it into a readily usable form for the workshop.

Alaskan yellow cedar also rates highly for use as ribs, but I have had no personal experience with it. The hardwoods normally used in boat construction—woods that bend so well and provide such fine support—are not acceptable in a canoe because of their weight and because once bent, they do not provide the necessary flexibility. Aside from the cedars, most softwoods do not bend well enough even when steamed to handle the sharp bends required in the construction of a canoe.

Planking

The picture is somewhat brighter when it comes to the planking. Here again most of the qualities demanded of the ribs are necessary with one notable exception: the planking does not have to be as severely bent longitudinally as the frames. White cedar is again the top contender for this job, but it is in extremely short supply in grades good enough and lengths long enough for planking a canoe. Although ideally one should use full-length planks to sheathe the hull, it is not necessary. The wide, flat ribs of a canoe make very good surfaces for placing beveled butt joints, which, if distributed sufficiently along the canoe, do not weaken the hull. Therefore, quality white cedar, even in lengths of 6 or 8 feet, is still the ideal material with which to plank a canoe.

Western red cedar is more readily available to most builders, often in clear long lengths with attractive vertical grain. It is somewhat more brittle than its eastern counterpart and will more readily split along the grain during the planking process, especially on tight areas of the canoe such as the turn of the bilge. The rot-resistant qualities of red cedar are likewise inferior to those of white cedar. Overall, however, red cedar is a very acceptable and beautiful planking material when applied with care. It is a rather expensive wood, but it is stocked by a large number of lumber wholesalers and retailers around the country. In addition, most commercially available clapboards are milled from this wood, and although they are cut on a bevel and often exceedingly dry, these can be milled out into suitable planking that will serve well enough if sufficiently soaked during the planking operation.

Clear white pine has been used for canoe planking, since it is relatively easy to obtain in clear lengths, but it is not nearly as satisfactory as either of the cedars. Spruce (either northern white, sometimes called eastern or native spruce, or Sitka) would make a tough sheathing, but it would be noticeably heavier and substantially less rot-resistant than cedar. Hardwoods are obviously eliminated because of their weight.

Gunwales

The gunwales or rails of the canoe are equally important, for they alone tie the whole structure together from end to end and distribute the stresses along the

Two white cedar strakes (foreground) contrasted with a western red cedar strake.

length of the canoe. They must be supple enough to take the complex sweeps along the sheer and strong enough to withstand great strains as the canoe works in rough water. They must also support the weight of the paddlers using the suspended seats and often the additional strain of an outboard motor clamped to a bracket on the side. And they must be light!

Northern white spruce, when available in clear stock of the appropriate length (which is just about never), is clearly the most satisfactory material I have used for this purpose. It withstands the complex bends and takes the relatively large fastenings even better than Sitka spruce. (The reason, however, may be only that the Sitka I have used was kiln dried while the "native" spruce was air dried.) Should you be fortunate enough to know a lumber retailer in your area who stocks house framing lumber from mills in northern New England, it would be worthwhile to persuade the dealer to let you look carefully through his stock. Most large mills in that area do not bother to grade structural lumber over 16 feet long, and with a lot of searching, it is sometimes possible to come up with whole long planks of clear eastern spruce. I have found lumber dealers by and large to be an unbelievably cooperative class of gentlemen who often bend over backward to help find suitable stock when they learn that your special project is the construction of some type of boat. As a group they have helped me out more often than I can remember, never charging me a premium for their extra effort.

Sitka spruce, my second choice, is commonly available in the clear grades required. Sitka rates very high among all woods in its excellent strength-to-weight ratio, which is such an important factor in canoe building.

This view shows the compound bends that make resilience an important requirement for any gunwale material.

Many canoe builders commonly use hardwood, particularly mahogany, for the outer gunwales. This is partly because the harder materials take abrasion and actual blows without nicking better than the spruce, and also because the darker woods contrast nicely with the otherwise blond shades of the interior. Good Honduras mahogany is definitely superior to the Philippine variety for this purpose. Ash or oak serves still better, and even some of the furniture woods can make a very durable, and certainly striking, outwale. I prefer to keep the weight down as much as possible in a canoe, however, and although my own 18′6″ White canoe has black cherry outer gunwales, my next canoe will have spruce rails inboard and out.

Should spruce of the required quality be absolutely impossible to obtain, there is no reason (other than the disadvantage of the increased weight) why hardwoods cannot be used for both gunwales. They make an attractive and durable (although rather stiff) sheer.

Stems

The stems, thwarts, seats, and decks, which constitute the remaining wooden portion of the canoe, are traditionally made from ash. Ash flexes well, and it is tough, light, and attractive when finished. In the case of the stems, it also bends well when steamed or boiled. However, ash is not the most rot-resistant wood available, and it is not uncommon to find the tips of the stems in older canoes to be either soft or even totally rotted away if they were not previously treated. White oak is a superior material for the stems, because its advantages in terms of rot resistance more than compensate for its slight extra weight.

Thwarts

Thwarts should also be made from oak or ash. Thwarts are important structural units of the canoe, and there should be no compromise in the material, since both these woods are readily available. Ash may well be the better choice for thwarts, because it is lighter and also more flexible, a factor that could prevent the gunwales from cracking under extreme stress.

Seats

The same woods are recommended for seat frames. It is possible to mill ash or oak down to reasonably light stock and still retain enough strength to support the paddler. The type of filler used also determines the size of the stock necessary. The prewoven natural cane fillers that are pressed into a groove routed into the frame are surprisingly durable, look neat, and have the advantage of not requiring through-holes in the frame as do all the actual woven alternatives. Therefore, it is possible to use slightly smaller stock to construct the frames. On the other hand, the actual lacing of nylon, neoprene, or natural rawhide or cane—carefully done— probably results in a more durable seat filler and can provide excellent comfort as well.

Many old-timers in northern Maine preferred the slat-type seat because the cedar or ash slats were durable and easy to replace. But these outdoorsmen must have come with tougher backsides than today's counterparts, because whatever was gained in durability was certainly sacrificed in comfort.

Decks and Keel

The breasthooks, which are always called the decks on a canoe, hold the two rails and the stem together at each end. The decks must hold fastenings well, because when the canoe is new, this area is constantly strained by the tendency of the gunwales to try to straighten out into their original form.

Ash is commonly used because of its ability to hold fastenings, but unfortunately, the moisture that accumulates around the tips when the canoe is stored upside down often causes the tip ends of the decks to rot after a time, along with the tops of the stems. Treating decks and stems with a quality wood preservative goes a long way toward preventing this rot, but if white oak is available, it would be wise to use it here in the first place.

To cut down on weight, spruce has often been used as a material for the decks. It too holds the fastenings surprisingly well, but without treatment, it does tend to turn punky in this semienclosed space.

The soundest decks I have seen in an old canoe were very thick crowned cedar affairs that, although in a well-used craft, appeared as sturdy as the day they were installed. It was a very short canoe, however, so the strain of the gunwales was minimized, and the decks were thick enough to hold extra-large screws. The decks had the further advantage of being light, despite their thickness.

The small outside keel, which increases the stability and tracking ability of canoes used primarily on open water, is best fashioned from oak or ash for obvious reasons.

Fastenings

In terms of fastenings, brass and bronze are surely the standard acceptable metals, although copper would be an excellent substitute. Aside from brass canoe tacks, sources of which I have listed in the appendix at the end of the book, most of the fastenings are not difficult to obtain.

The ideal canoe tack as depicted in the figure is $^{11}/_{16}$ or $^{3}/_{4}$ inch long and has a fairly light shank and a very thin, sharp tip for turning back into the wood (clinching). Although a completely flat head is acceptable, a slightly rounded head allows the tack to be driven farther into the planking with less of a "hammer blossom" effect during clinching. A similar tack made of copper would also be excellent, but most that I have seen have been too thick and do not have a sharp enough tip, which would cause unnecessary splitting of the $^{5}/_{32}$-inch planking.

For securing the ribs to the outboard side of the inwale, $^{3}/_{4}$-inch or $^{7}/_{8}$-inch 14-gauge silicon bronze ringed boat nails are excellent in terms of holding power as well as durability. Should these be impossible to find, 1-inch galvanized box nails, or better yet, galvanized ring nails, will serve adequately. The screws that later secure the outside rail to the canoe reinforce their function anyway.

Similar fastenings can be used to fasten the very ends of the planking to the stems. A slightly smaller bronze ring nail is better for this job because it is less likely to split the stem. But these $^{5}/_{8}$-inch 16-gauge beauties are extremely difficult to obtain. Very small $^{5}/_{8}$-inch steel nails are often used for this purpose and seem to hold everything together, even though on most old canoes I have dissected, the heads appear to be completely rusted away.

The outer gunwales are best secured with $1^{1}/_{2}$-inch or $1^{3}/_{4}$-inch No. 8 bronze or brass flathead wood screws, whereas the optional outside keel is fastened by $1^{1}/_{4}$-inch No. 10 screws of the same material, with brass finishing washers to prevent them from burrowing too deeply into the cedar frames.

The seats and thwarts are bolted to the inside rail with $^{1}/_{4}$-inch or $^{3}/_{16}$-inch bronze carriage bolts or with $^{3}/_{16}$-inch round-headed brass machine screws, combined with the appropriate finish washers. These will vary in length from $2^{1}/_{4}$ inches for at-

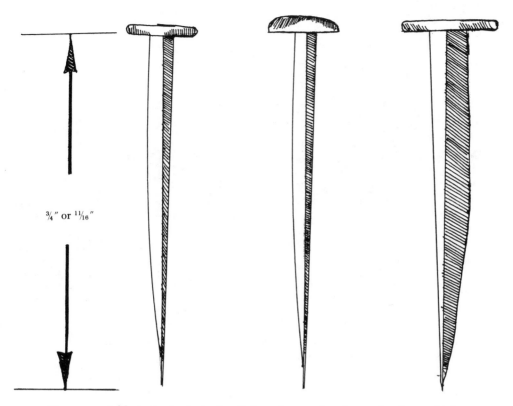

¾″ or ¹¹⁄₁₆″

Two acceptable tacks for fastening (left and center) and one that is too thick.

A thick cedar deck that is attractive and almost totally rot-resistant.

Various fastenings used in canoe construction: bronze carriage bolts, bronze screws, brass canoe tacks, bronze ring nails, and brass finishing washers.

taching the thwarts to 3½ inches for hanging the bow seat the proper distance below the gunwales.

Canvas and Fillers

The appropriate weight of the cotton duck canvas to cover the hull is best determined by the intended use of the canoe. Naturally, the heavier the material, the more durable the covering and the resulting overall strength of the canoe. The relative weight of the cloth is designated by numbers, which decrease as the canvas gets heavier. Normally No. 8 or No. 10 canvas is stretched over canoes intended for normal to heavy general use. If the canoe is to be used predominantly in areas where rapids are frequently encountered, properly filled and finished No. 8 duck is a good choice. No. 6 would be even stronger, and on a canoe used almost exclusively for expedition work, it would be highly recommended. However, the weight of such a skin would be substantial, so it is important not to use a heavier cloth than necessary. No. 10 canvas is perfectly suitable for general use, including moderate white-water work. No. 12 canvas should be reserved for canoes under 16 feet intended for use on lakes, ponds, and quiet streams, and wherever weight is the primary consideration, such as on a canoe intended primarily for backpacking into beaver flowages.

Cotton duck canvas in sufficient widths is normally available from awning dealers, art supply houses, and most marine supply dealers. Avoid poor-quality canvas, which displays numerous burrs or obvious runs across the weave.

The traditional white lead-based canvas filler has been largely replaced by new commercial mixtures with an oil base. These new fillers increase the waterproof efficiency of the covering and are less likely to crack. Besides waterproofing the hull, the functions of these specialized fillers are to provide a tough, smooth surface for paint, to resist abrasion, and to add overall strength to the wood-canvas system. Many builders have their own special formulas for mixing up fillers, but fillers are available commercially from a number of sources listed in the appendix.

Other Materials

A quality clear wood preservative is another important material to have on hand. Treating each piece of wood in the craft with such a solution can greatly extend the life of the wood, and the best preservatives completely saturate the grain and do not interfere with the normal finishing of the wood.

Paints and varnishes and their application are discussed in a later chapter. These products or their substitutes are readily available in most areas.

An Unhappy Canoeist

The small patch of carapace sticking above the mud scarcely indicated the bulk of the snapping turtle to which it belonged. But by the time I had it by the tail, and swung it into the canoe, it was too late to reconsider. With uncharacteristic speed, it lunged for Doug, who had been an innocent bystander in the middle of the canoe. Doug leaped forward with unprecedented agility, landing in the bow on Harry's lap. Then the snapper drove me onto the stern seat, taking my measure with cold, reptilian eyes and hissing menacingly, while opening and closing his lethal jaws. He finally crawled up into the stem and attempted an exit through the bottom. It took all my strength to pull his claws free from the cant ribs and toss him back into the ooze from whence he had emerged.

5

Special Equipment

In addition to the actual canoe form, the canoe builder can employ a wide assortment of special tools, equipment, and jigs to make his task simpler and more efficient. Much of this equipment consists of customized designs tailored to the needs of the individual builder or shop, and a good deal of it can be regarded as more trouble than it is worth to someone planning to build a canoe or two in the home workshop, where labor-saving devices are not critical. However, most of this equipment and its applications are of interest to anyone getting involved with this craft, so I will describe some of the devices, explain their applications, and attempt to help the amateur decide whether or not a particular piece will be worth his time and effort either to build or to procure.

Basic Tools

Before beginning discussion of these extraordinary aids, it is first necessary to list the tools and equipment that are considered essential or standard. In rural Maine, where a disproportionate number of part- and full-time canoe builders live, one can find as many levels of mechanization as philosophies on what constitutes a suitable canoe. The workshops range from made-over woodsheds (where canoe-building activities may occasionally take a back seat to small engine repair or snow-sled customizing) to Old Town's efficient, modernized operation beneath their immense plastic fabrication factory. There is no direct correlation between the quality of the finished product and the amount of equipment in the shop. I think it is safe to say, however, that most woodworkers can achieve the same results in less time if they are properly equipped, and that a minimal amount of woodworking equipment is necessary for all but the most resourceful craftsmen.

Milling capability is an essential consideration, because the builder has little use for standard dimensional stock. Virtually every piece of wood going into the craft

51

will have to be sawn, planed, sanded, dadoed, or shaped. Therefore, unless he can rely on a custom woodworking shop in his vicinity, a prospective builder must be prepared to deal with this reality. A table saw can be considered essential. Most of them have the capability of handling a dado system as well as a stationary sanding disk. Fitted with a fine-toothed carbide blade, such a saw is capable of resawing the planking and ribs from thicker stock, leaving surfaces smooth enough to be directly sanded and eliminating the absolute necessity of a thickness planer. The planer, however, can do a faster and generally better job, and if one is available, it will expedite the milling operation; it is a must for any production work.

Some type of power sanding unit will also be a great aid. Standard types that the builder will find useful include stationary disk and belt units, hand-held power-belt sanders, and portable orbital machines with a long, flat base. In order to get a fine finished product, it is essential to sand all the interior surfaces of the planking and frames before the canoe goes together. The interior of the finished canoe is too complex and difficult to sand properly once it is built. If time is a consideration, the various stationary-belt machines are of tremendous help in accomplishing the presanding. Another good alternative is a sanding disk that fits the arbor of the table saw and can be used in conjunction with the ripping fence. This allows the builder control to ensure uniform thickness of the stock. Surpassing all these alternatives for general usefulness is the rather specialized large drum sander, which is described later in this chapter.

A routing unit is used to mold the edges of the ribs; it can also dado the outer gunwales and shape or relieve the edges of gunwales, thwarts, and seats. However, virtually the same effect can be achieved on the basic table saw in combination with the sanding equipment already discussed. The hand-held router is perhaps the most versatile and therefore the most useful of the options in this department, and having access to one can be helpful, although it is not altogether necessary.

A bandsaw or a good-quality hand-held sabersaw is normally used for cutting out decks and thwarts, and it can be useful for a variety of other functions throughout the construction. I would consider someone without access to one or the other to be at a decided disadvantage in tackling the project.

Turning away from the complex power units, which our experienced forefathers did so commendably without, we can now list the hand tools that should be accessible to the prospective builder. These include a claw hammer (preferably a small tack variety), various screwdrivers, a brace, a utility knife with replaceable blades, a chalkline, a block plane (with a reasonably low cutting angle), an electric or hand drill with an assortment of wood bits, a chisel or two, at least a dozen 4-inch or larger C-clamps, an adjustable wrench, and, when the time finally arrives, a paintbrush and a proper varnish brush.

An assortment of sandpaper of various grits will be necessary for the sanding tools already mentioned and for hand sanding.

Specialized Tools

The specialized devices that I will now describe can be divided into three categories: (1) large power equipment and the accessories and adaptations

A hand-held router can be mounted on a surface to make an effective shaping unit.

associated with it, (2) tools, both power and hand, that can be readily purchased from dealers but might not be found around the average home workshop, and (3) highly specialized tools, jigs, and equipment that will have to be made or at least adapted from existing materials.

Power Tools and Accessories

I will take the space to describe only one major piece of specialized power equipment that is essential to any production shop but unnecessary for the amateur—the heavy-duty drum sander. I doubt whether these are any longer available commercially, if indeed they ever were. The one we are fortunate enough to have was built by a resourceful and very skilled craftsman, and it has so many applications around the woodworking shop that it is well worth describing. The basis of the unit is a revolving cylinder, 16 inches in diameter by 11 inches wide, driven by a 1½ h.p. motor. The drum itself is hollow, constructed of beveled spruce staves screwed to a ½-inch circular piece of plywood at each end. A metal coupling plate to attach the drum to the shaft is secured to each plywood end, and coupling, plywood, and stave ends alike are covered by an additional ½-inch circular plywood end panel, which has a square hole routed into the middle to expose the heads of the machine screws on the coupling plate itself.

One stave is intentionally recessed and backed up by a tapped and threaded hardwood strut, forming a groove designed to accommodate the overlapping ends of the abrasive, and a predrilled section of brass half-round stock, which holds the XHD cloth onto the surface of the drum. The wooden surface of the cylinder is cushioned with a layer of rubber-backed carpet, which is glued onto the staves. Quarter-inch flathead machine bolts, threaded into the hardwood strut, hold the brass half-round and ultimately the cloth in place.

The base of the unit is constructed of maple, bolted together and designed to suspend the drum on its shaft above and at an angle from the power source. The shaft turns inside the heavy-duty bearings located on the framework on either side of the drum. On one side, inboard of the bearing, a pulley receives the belt that transfers the force from the electric motor.

The machine is simplicity at its finest, providing maximum efficiency with a bare minimum of moving parts. It is especially useful for presanding the planking and ribs; but with familiarity it can be applied to a variety of jobs around any woodshop.

One adaptation that is used with a table saw to expedite the job of cutting tapers on the ends of the ribs is a homemade device that utilizes the principle of a sliding wedge to push the ribs, several at a time, past the saw blade at a constant angle. This device is constructed of hardwood, and it bolts to the fence of the saw unit. A double-beveled track along its length matches a corresponding groove on the wooden slide that holds the wedge. The rip fence with the jig bolted to it is set the desired distance from the blade, and from two to five ribs stacked atop one another against the head of the wedge sit at an angle to the blade. When the ribs are pushed ahead, the taper is automatically cut. Although this is an interesting device, I doubt whether the work saved would merit constructing one just to build an occasional canoe. On the other hand, as a labor-saver in a production shop, the simple device is extremely effective.

Another accessory that can help the builder get the most out of a piece of power machinery is a shaper-molder head, which can be used on a table saw or radial arm saw. These heads are usually manufactured by the maker of the saw and essentially convert the saw into a stationary shaping machine. Most have removable blades, which can be replaced with a variety of shaped cutters that allow the saw to perform a wide range of shaping, molding, and sanding jobs. However, in the canoe shop, its primary use is for shaping the edges of the ribs.

The recessed brass half-round holds the abrasive cloth in place.

The author's home-built drum sanding unit.

A sliding wooden wedge for cutting uniform tapers on the ends of the ribs.

A shaping/molding head in place on a radial arm saw. (P.H. DesLauriers)

Commercially Available Tools and Aids

The second category of special tools and equipment consists of tools that are available from dealers but are not commonly found around the home workshop. A small clawed tack hammer is practically a necessity. Conventional carpenter's hammers are so clumsy and heavy for such light work that they not only are frustrating to use but also can easily damage the light planking material.

Although a straight-bladed standard utility knife is adequate for cutting the light planking, many builders prefer a conventional hooked linoleum knife for this job. Actually I find the knife more useful if the blade has been ground or filed down a bit as shown in the illustration. The very small planes for model making are likewise very useful and far more enjoyable to use in the planking operation than

Some hand tools useful for canoe building. From left: Hardwood wedge used to keep plank-ing from splitting when tacks are driven; a combination square; a clinching iron; a tack puller; a modeling plane; a linoleum knife; and a tack hammer.

the much heavier standard block planes. As with conventional planes, the low-angle miniplanes are preferable to the deep-cutting, high-angle variety.

A standard tack puller is another very useful item that must be included in the inventory before beginning the project. Upholsterer's or artist's canvas-stretching pliers, which are available from art supply houses, are very helpful in achieving a properly stretched canvas covering. Another version of this tool is the flat-jawed vise-grip, which can do the same job and may be a little easier on hands unaccustomed to the strenuous work. A come-along—or better still, a small hand-operated winch—is necessary for pulling the dry canvas taut horizontally during the canvas operation.

Jigs and Molds

Finally, in the special tool category, we have the small square-based, multidirectional or orbital sanding machine. This compact power unit, when used in conjunction with the optional foam pad base, is an excellent device for finish sanding the ribs inside the canoe before sealing and varnishing. No matter how carefully

A small hand-operated winch for pulling canvas taut along the canoe hull.

the frames have been presanded, the subsequent steam-bending and construction processes are bound to raise the grain slightly as well as soil and nick the wood to some degree.

The wood-canvas canoe is truly the child of ingenuity. Through the years the production of these marvelous craft has led to the development of a wide variety of jigs and aids that expedite the construction process. The solid building form, discussed earlier, is the greatest achievement in facilitating the production of the

This jig for prebending the ash stems is wide enough to accommodate stems for two canoes.

A simple jig for prebending the ends of the gunwales after steaming.

nearly identical canoes on a large scale. Several smaller accomplishments also played their parts in rendering the building process more manageable.

Jigs for prebending the hardwood stems and the compound bends at the ends of the gunwales represent two such necessities. The ash or oak stems are prebent after steaming. Since a relatively flat piece of wood bends more easily without twisting to the side than a perfectly square piece or one that is thicker than it is wide, a jig is normally constructed to accommodate stock a bit more than twice the width of the finished stem. After the bent stock has dried and hardened into the intended shape, it is taken off the jig and split on the table saw, and the two identical pieces are then beveled and notched appropriately.

The jig itself is constructed of a wooden frame that matches exactly the shape of the stem of the canoe, sandwiched between two identically shaped pieces of ½-inch plywood. The thickness of the internal frame stock is determined by the number of pairs of stems the builder wishes to bend during one steaming. Pairs of wooden tabs strategically placed along the curve are provided with through-holes that allow a bolt to slide through over the bent stock. Wedges driven under these bolts hold the wet stock snugly against the form.

The same principle applies to forms constructed to prebend the ends of the gunwales. Canoes with dramatic sheer lines that sweep upward sharply at the ends while at the same time pulling in to the centerline from a fairly wide beam present a real test of a gunwale's resilience. Often it is physically impossible for the wood to

This steam box, built of cedar, is large enough to accommodate the ribs for two canoes. It is attached to blocks for easy elevation when not in use.

take the compound curves without first steam-bending one of the sweeps into the rail. For this purpose, builders have developed jigs similar to the stem forms mentioned above. The photo details the construction of such a form; cleats can be added the proper distance on the crosspieces to form a channel that prevents the premilled gunwales from twisting while being bent. The steam-softened gunwales are secured to the crosspieces by C-clamps, as shown in the photo on page 61.

The steam box or chamber is very important, but basically it is simply any wooden or metal enclosure into which the stock can be placed and the steam introduced. The cedar steam box in the illustration is a very useful unit for a small-scale commercial operation; it will hold enough ribs for two complete canoes. For the amateur project, a less sophisticated box will serve just as well.

Wood is a very good material for constructing a chamber, but galvanized sheet metal works just as well. Some provision should be made for separating the stock and exposing as much surface to the steam as possible. In the case of a metal chamber, it is important to ensure that the wood does not lie directly on the surface of the metal, where it is more likely to bake than to become saturated with steam.

It is not necessary to build the steam chamber large enough to accommodate all the ribs at the same time. Steam-bending can be accomplished in stages, or a new rib can be inserted each time one is taken out and should soften sufficiently by the time you get around to using it.

A view of the interior of the steam box shows the vertical dowels that separate the ribs, allowing better exposure to the steam.

A converted galvanized water heater on a metal stand, fired by a propane torch, makes a good setup for boiling stem stock, but good ventilation must be maintained.

The source of steam can be almost anything. All that is required is an enclosed vessel, a heat source, and some provision for channeling the resulting steam into the chamber. The propane-fired plumber's torch in the photo, coupled with the stainless steel milking machine pail, is effective but must be used in a well-ventilated area. A kettle of water on a woodstove is perfectly adequate for the rib-bending operation, as is an open fire outdoors, sheltered from the wind.

The ash stem pieces and the ends of the rails require a much greater volume of steam for softening than do the easily bent cedar ribs. The outfit already described can be used to accomplish this task, but to ensure a higher degree of success, we resort to boiling the ash and spruce in a converted galvanized hot-water heater, using the same heat source. The metal tank is open at the top on one end, fitted with a sliding cover, and supported by a metal sawbuck (see illustration). It is possible to boil the ribs also, but the grain of the cedar will be raised drastically, and the wood is likely to stain, requiring a great deal more finish sanding than if the ribs were steam-bent.

Once again I will stress that ingenuity goes a long way toward solving this particular problem. Just keep in mind that the only requirements are a source of steam and an enclosed space.

A long fairing block is a useful aid in preparing the already formed ribs for planking. Even the most careful bending jobs on the best of forms will result in a few slightly lifted rib edges that are out of tune with the smooth lines desirable on

A long block such as this one, surfaced with floor-sanding paper, is used to prepare the ribs for planking.

your finished canoe. Although generally these edges are not a serious problem, to achieve the fairest hull possible, it is helpful to go over the frames with this device to bring any minor inconsistencies into line. Surfaced with 40-grit floor-sanding paper, the block is moved horizontally along the backs of the ribs and then vertically to achieve maximum fairness. This process is covered in more detail in the appropriate section of the book. To be effective, the block itself must be long enough so that the base spans three or four ribs at one time. The ends of the base should curve up enough to keep them from snagging on the ribs, and it should be built of a light material, such as cedar, with a grip that is comfortable to the hand.

An indispensable tool—to the production shop at least—is a heavy metal clinching iron used on the inside of the canoe to turn the tips of the tacks back into the wood. Clinching is necessary to ensure that the fastenings are tight and the heads are recessed properly into the outside surface of the planking, even when the process has been started by the steel bands on the form. The iron is held against the inside surface of the rib while the builder drives the tack home with the tack hammer. The better models are hollow, giving the builder a firm grip, and they have a wide variety of surfaces and angles for matching the various contours of the interior hull. The one pictured in the figure is of cast polished steel; it is designed to be effective even in the difficult-to-reach recesses at the ends of the canoe.

Obviously such a tool is not available on the standard tool market, but the same function can be accomplished by improvising with a variety of metal shapes. Metal

The ideal clinching iron is hollow for lightness and to provide a firm grip. It is shaped to match the various contours inside the canoe.

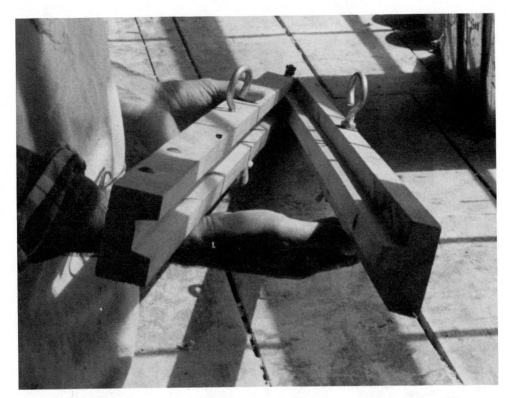

Although these stretching clamps are nicely tongue-and-grooved, a one-time setup need not be quite as fancy.

hammers, ball peens, mallets, and axe heads will serve if used carefully. Any metal object with a sharp edge must be used with great care to avoid nicking or crushing the wood. The tools used by auto body mechanics to remove dents in metal are similar in concept, and they can make good substitutes. I have heard of using smooth flat and rounded stones on limited repair projects, and this concept might present another possibility.

The canvasing operation requires two more specialized devices. Wooden stretching clamps are designed to grip the folded duck securely while it is suspended during the canvasing process. These clamps should be 40 inches long and constructed of hardwood for a production operation, but softwood 2 x 4's are fine for occasional amateur use. The more sophisticated clamps are hinged at the top to open and close like jaws, and they have a tongue-and-groove alignment system, which also ensures a firmer grip on the canvas. For a one-time stand, none of this is necessary; the canvas is simply placed between the two lengths of wood, which are then held firmly together by C-clamps. The stretching clamps are hung by chain lengths from the overhead of the shop, or perhaps the branches of existing trees outdoors. The "professional" version closes tightly by means of bolts at either end of the rig and perhaps one C-clamp in the middle of the stretcher. Double eyebolts, as

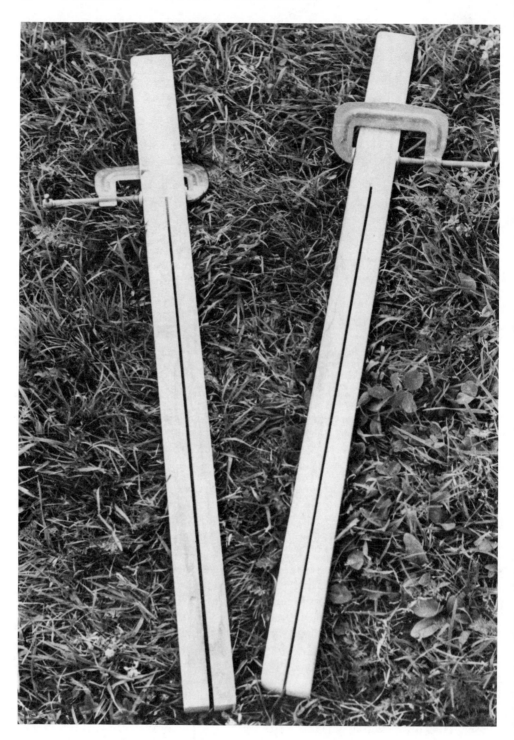

The giant "clothespins" used for canvasing the canoe.

illustrated, allow the clamps to be secured horizontally to a beam or solid structure on one end and to the winch or come-along on the other; but it is nearly as effective simply to attach the chains or cables directly to the C-clamp in the middle.

Also helpful in the canvasing process are a pair of large "clothespins," which can be made by splitting a 2½-foot length of ash or oak about two-thirds of the way up its length and preventing further splitting by placing a small bolt just above the split or even putting a clamp in the same spot. These clothespin devices hold the canvas against the sides of the canoe for tacking at the extreme ends, where otherwise it would tend to pull away from the canoe.

This completes the basic list of unique tools and aids that will help the canoe builder. The best method for determining exactly which tools will apply to a particular situation is to gather the ones that can be readily acquired or built and add others as they become necessary. Only by this method can you properly gauge the value of each option to the overall execution of the job.

Beyond Ambition

"You got to file a saw for every canoe to get that thin planking. Cedar looks easy to saw but it's really the hardest thing on a saw that there is. In fact, I think the gravel has growed right up into it. I get rail spruce 21 feet long. I don't splice my rails.

"I found them out in the four foot, being cut up, clear spruce. I hired a truck, went down and got them sawed for me. Clear spruce 21 feet is hard to get because there aren't any more of those trees. They got to be the outside of those nice white spruce. These younger trees has grown up—might be 21 feet, but there will be pin knots in them somewheres. For rails, you want clear spruce. Nothing so strong as spruce rails. Mahogany don't hardly hold together.

"There's a lot more to making a canoe than just ambition."

Myron Smart
in an interview with Lynn Franklin

6

Preparing the Stock

Having gathered the various materials and made other necessary preparations, the builder will be ready to prepare his stock for the actual construction. The machinery has been cleaned, sharpened, and oiled, the wood is dry, and only a bit of initiative is necessary to launch the project officially.

Milling out stock can be tedious and even exhausting work. It should never be hurried. Careful attention is mandatory throughout the operation to ensure the operator's safety and a gratifying finished product. The following description applies specifically to building an 18′ 6″ White guide canoe from materials gathered as they became available in Maine. The builder choosing a different model with different accessories and utilizing stock of varying dimensions will have to adapt his procedures accordingly.

Stems

The ash or oak stem stock seems like a reasonable place to begin. The rough stock is just an inch thick and is several inches wider than the piece desired. Quarter-sawn stock would be ideal for this purpose, because the chances of its exhibiting the desirable grain structure are much greater. It is more reasonable to expect to find plain-sawn stock, however, unless the wood is specially procured from a custom lumber retailer.

Having tried all patterns of grain, and seldom achieved the same results twice, I have never been able to arrive at any definite conclusions regarding just which pattern is ideal for actual bending. However, I have discovered two grain patterns that are *not* ideal. When viewed from the edge of the stock, grain that runs off the stock at a relatively sharp angle, or grain lines that are unusually close together, even though apparently straight, have a poor chance of success in the bending operation. Otherwise, there seems to be little correlation, and any stick with the grain running more or less up the edge of it, as long as the lines are not too compressed together, is reasonably likely to bend successfully. If the grain meanders off the stock predominantly in one direction, it is advisable to make that side the inside surface of the intended curve.

To ensure as little sanding as possible in the future, and to true up the edges a bit, the first step is to run the stock through the table saw to get two good milled edges. The carbide-tipped blade will dress these edges very neatly, almost as though the piece had passed through the planer. If the stock is particularly crooked, it may be necessary to strike a line or draw one with a straightedge, cut it by eye, and then true it with either a power or hand jointer before running the second edge past the saw. The length of the stock should correspond to the stem of the canoe, allowing at least three or four extra inches. The finished stems, where they are not altered by beveling or shaping, will be molded ⅞ inch and sided ¹³⁄₁₆ inch (here *molding* refers to the vertical dimension of the stock and *siding* to the flat or horizontal dimension). Therefore, since we wish to bend the stems as one unit, the width of the stock necessary will measure exactly two inches to allow for cutting the piece in half and sanding.

The next step is planing this piece to ⅞ inch thickness. I am using the singular in describing this process, but the prudent builder will have one or even two spares ready so the operation will not be stalled if the first piece fails the bending test. After planing, the stem stock should be placed in a reasonably damp place until a couple of days prior to the actual bending, at which time the stock should be submerged in water. Leaving ash in water more than two days tends to discolor or at least darken the wood.

Gunwales

The inside and outside gunwales of the canoe can be ripped from the stock together, although they will require separate preparation after this initial step. In order to have a little leeway, a 20-foot plank is just about right for the 18′6″ White. Assuming the stock is 1¾-inch-thick structural lumber, it will be necessary to make two cuts to get the 1³⁄₁₆-inch-square strips from the rough planks. The first cut slices a strip of this width from the plank with a molded dimension of the original 1¾ inches.

If the shop has no provision for handling offcuts, it will be advantageous to set up a slide or roller system to help manage the ungainly, ever-lengthening lumber that emerges from the other end of the saw. Otherwise it is nearly impossible to handle the operation with any degree of accuracy or safety. Two lengths of plywood, two feet in width, tacked to sawhorses, or one strip coupled with a portable roller platform, will serve very well. If you feel uneasy holding such an unmanageable piece against the fence for ripping, you can use a featherboard to help hold it evenly to the saw. The featherboard will have to be reset each time a slice is ripped from the original stock.

Next, with the fence set the same distance from the saw, the strips are cut square by turning them 90 degrees onto their flat surface and sending them through the

The surfaces of the gunwales are sanded before they are placed on the form.

saw once again. Since these strips are limber and are of consistent width, it is advisable to set up a featherboard to help keep the cuts uniform.

The inwales for the White canoe are molded 1¹⁄₁₆ inches and sided 1 inch even. The sides are square, since the design displays neither flare nor tumblehome, either of which would require an appropriate bevel on the outboard side of the inner gunwale, and a corresponding one on the outer gunwale as well. In this case, however, the inwales are next planed to the finished dimension in the thickness planer. The outer gunwales are also molded 1¹⁄₁₆ inches, but the sided dimension is only ¹⁵⁄₁₆ inch before rabbeting. The gunwales, cut to size, are clamped to a long bench and all surfaces are presanded with a fine-grit belt on a portable belt sander.

For a canoe with noticeable tumblehome built into the design, the process would vary as follows. First, the amount of bevel would have to be determined by actually measuring it on the form or on the original canoe. This is done with a sliding bevel gauge, as shown in the illustration. Since the amount of tumblehome tends to vary along the length of the sheer, which usually is greatest amidships and practically disappears near the ends, it is necessary to determine an average angle somewhere in the quarters of the canoe. The resulting bevel, as indicated by the gauge, can be used to determine the necessary tilt of the blade. The inwales to be beveled are first planed to the correct molded dimension and to the maximum sided dimension, as with the square gunwales. All but the outboard sides are sanded; then, on the table saw, the correct bevel is cut on this side the whole length of the

A bevel is used to determine the amount of tumblehome on the form.

The rabbet in the outer gunwale is cut with a dado head on a table saw. Note the use of a guide and featherboard to ensure a uniform cut. (P.H. DesLauriers)

inwale. Great care must be taken to make this cut uniform; use a featherboard to hold the inwale into the fence and a horizontal strip clamped to the fence itself to hold the stock flush on the table top.

The outside gunwales are first planed and sanded to the proper dimension, whether or not they will require a bevel. In either case the inboard surface will be rabbeted, leaving a ¼-inch-deep lip along the top. The lip fits over the sheer plank and rests neatly against the back side of the ribs. The rabbeting process is best accomplished on the table saw, using a dado unit wide enough to take all the material away—approximately ¼ inch with one pass. On a straight-sided gunwale such as the type on the White, the dado blade remains vertical and is set at a height ¼ inch lower than the molded dimension of 1 1/16 inches. Position the fence so that exactly ¼ inch of material will be removed by the saw from the sided dimension. When a test section confirms the setup, install a featherboard to hold the stock to the fence and a horizontal guide to prevent it from lifting; then simply run the two gunwales through.

On a gunwale requiring a beveled inside surface, the setup is similar, except that the blade is set at the proper angle. Also, because the inboard surface of the lip must be slightly beveled with a block or miniplane to match the angle on the remainder of the surface, it is necessary to remove 5/16 inch of material from the stock instead of ¼ inch on the straight-sided gunwale, thus providing the extra material on the lip to be worked off (see figure).

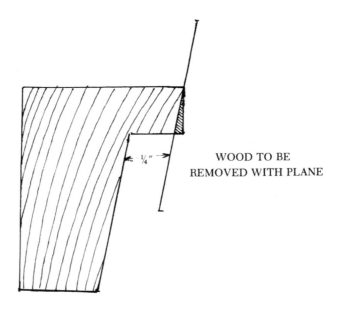

WOOD TO BE
REMOVED WITH PLANE

¼″

OUTER GUNWALE

Lip on gunwale is beveled to match corresponding bevel.

The only remaining work on the gunwales is to taper the ends of the inwales from full width to ¼ inch to give the canoe a more graceful appearance at the ends. First cut these "rails" to the proper length as determined by actual measurement along the sheer. The inwale should actually be trimmed two inches longer than the maximum length anticipated. The material should be removed from the outboard surface of the inwales, leaving the inside surface smooth and consistent to facilitate joining it to the decks.

Mark the 20-inch taper on the ends of the gunwale, allowing ¼ inch of material to be left at the tip. Then cut well outside the mark on either the table saw or the bandsaw and finish right to the mark with a block plane. The taper may appear abrupt and angular, but when the gunwale is bent into the canoe, the result is a pleasing natural reduction, lending an air of lightness and elegance to the appearance of the bows.

Planking

Milling out planking material is nobody's idea of a good time, but unfortunately it is a necessary step in proceeding toward a finished canoe. I have previously estimated the amount of stock I will need by figuring the surface area of an open rectangular box matching roughly the maximum dimensions of the canoe. The box ends up being 19 feet long by 3 feet wide by 2 feet deep. The area of the largest sur-

Cutting the 20-inch taper at the end of the gunwales.

Smoothing the gunwale taper with a block plane.

face is 57 square feet. The two sides total 76 square feet more, and the combined surface of the ends is 12 square feet, giving a total of 145 square feet. Since I can resaw my 1-inch stock into three $\frac{5}{32}$-inch-thick planks, I determine that I will need one-third of 145, or 48 board feet. Since the stock is of exceptional quality, there will be little that cannot be used, and this figure should be adequate, even taking into account what will be broken or otherwise discarded in the planking process.

The white cedar rough stock I am using measures 1″ x 3¼″ and is in clear lengths of 6 feet and 8 feet. Since all surfaces are rough, it is necessary to trim up the edges to get a consistent width and to make sure the planks will fit together tightly. Planking that is not absolutely consistent in width can lead to a nightmarish planking experience; at each joint it will result in a little step along a run that should be perfectly straight. Therefore run both edges of the rough stock past the blade in two distinct steps, to produce stock exactly three inches in width.

This dimension, coincidentally, is the maximum height to which the blade on most 10-inch table saws can be raised. It must be raised to this height in order to proceed to the next step, which is resawing the 1-inch stock into three ¼-inch-thick planks. The ¼-inch dimension allows the builder to do the resawing job in two steps and leaves plenty of material to plane the rough surfaces of the planks smoothly.

I choose to resaw my planks without the aid of a featherboard so I can complete each board as I come to it, making two passes and reducing it to three thin planks. If you want the help of a featherboard, however, it is possible to go completely through the pile of stock and make the first cut, then reset the tension and go through a second time to make the final cut. A ¼-inch-thick push stick provides a measure of safety when pushing the end of the planking past the blade.

The planking is next run through the thickness planer at a bit over the desired $\frac{5}{32}$ inch to allow for sanding. The thickness of the planking can be altered within certain limits to accommodate special requirements. For example, a short canoe designed primarily for backpacking into quiet waters can be adequately sheathed with ⅛-inch planking, provided the paddler is aware of this slightly frailer construction. Likewise, $\frac{3}{16}$-inch planking might be in order for a large guide canoe intended primarily for expedition-type work on heavy water.

Sanding the planed surface of the stock is the final step in preparing the planking. It is next to impossible to accomplish this once the canoe is built, so this pre-sanding is especially important. The stationary drum sander described in the previous chapter accomplishes the job with speed and ease. It is used with XHD close coat abrasive cloth in the following manner. Step up to the unit and, gripping the plank about two-thirds of the way down with your right hand, place the planed side across the top of the revolving cylinder. Use the palm of your left hand to hold the limber plank to the abrasive drum, and draw the top half between your palm and the cylinder with a steady, arcing motion of your right hand. With fresh abrasive cloth, two such passes are usually sufficient. Then turn the plank end for end and treat the remaining half in the same manner. If the planing job was adequate, you can easily sand two or three planks in one minute's time.

This, of course, is not the only method of sanding the planks. The slightly tilted surface of a stationary belt sanding unit can be used similarly, provided the grit is not too coarse. Even a hand-held machine with a fine-grit belt can adequately sand

Resawing the planking from three-inch-wide stock approaches the very limits of the 10-inch blade's capacity.

Presanding the supple planking on the drum sander.

planking that is clamped onto a bench. Whatever method you choose, it is important to remember that the aim is to finish the surface of the planking without
noticeably or unevenly changing its thickness.

Ribs

Preparing the ribs is the most formidable milling job, one that involves many steps.
The finished ribs measure $2\frac{3}{8}$ inches wide by $\frac{5}{16}$ inch thick, and the width
diminishes in a taper at the very ends to about $1\frac{3}{4}$ inches. The frames are uniform in
thickness throughout their length, although in some old designs, including White's,
the ribs also diminished in thickness as they approached the sheer—sometimes
from $\frac{5}{16}$ inch down to $\frac{3}{16}$ inch. The edges are shaped and the primary surface sanded smooth before the ribs are steam-bent into shape.

The white cedar stock is rough-sawn, measuring 1 inch thick by $3\frac{1}{4}$ inches wide
by 60 inches long. To achieve two milled edges, run the stock through the table saw
twice, until the material is the desired $2\frac{3}{8}$ inches wide. Next, split each board on the
table saw to yield two ribs $\frac{7}{16}$ inch thick, and plane these to the desired $\frac{5}{16}$-inch
thickness. You must then cut the frames to the proper length to correspond to their
positions in the canoe. (This information must be obtained beforehand.) The
length of any given rib should be from 1 to 4 inches greater than the girth of the
canoe at that particular point. This margin makes it possible to use one length of rib
for several adjacent locations, simplifying the milling and steam-bending operations. Altogether, one can expect to deal with about 15 different rib lengths in
building a typical double-ended canoe with a total of 45 ribs. It is prudent to include a few spares of varying lengths, especially those near the tight bends at the
ends, to replace any that may be broken in the steaming operation.

Once the ribs have been trimmed to the proper lengths, the little tapering device
mentioned earlier comes into play. This sliding wedge, attached to the rip fence of
the saw unit, is unexcelled for cutting the 10-inch-long taper at each end of the rib;
the resulting frames measure only $1\frac{3}{4}$ inches in width at the ends.

The amateur can achieve the same result satisfactorily by individually marking
and cutting the taper on the bandsaw or table saw. Once again the taper may appear harsh and angular when viewed by itself, but when it is shaped, sanded, and
bent into the craft, the effect is very pleasing.

Next, use the drum sander to sand the best surface, in the same manner as the
planking. The edges of the ribs are generally shaped or beveled for aesthetic as well
as functional reasons. The blunted edges catch less and are less likely to be chipped,
split, or bruised. This effect can be achieved by simply beveling the frames on the
table saw, then softening the corners by sanding. The shape can also be molded by
a shaping or routing unit. Lacking the good fortune to own a stationary shaping
unit, I have come to depend on a molding head unit that adapts to the radial arm
saw. This accessory, described in the previous chapter, holds three cutting blades
and is set up with a specially designed fence that bolts onto the surface of the radial
arm saw bench, holds the stock at the proper angle to the cutter, and protects the
operator from an unguarded menace (see figure on page 85). I simply hold the
stock to the cutters and slide the piece along its whole length. A bit of practice is

Ripping the cedar stock to the proper 2⅜-inch width. Both edges should be milled.

Planing the rib stock to ⁵⁄₁₆ inch with a thickness planer.

Using the sliding wedge device to taper the ends of the ribs. (P.H. DesLauriers)

Sanding the rib stock. (P.H. DesLauriers)

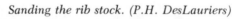

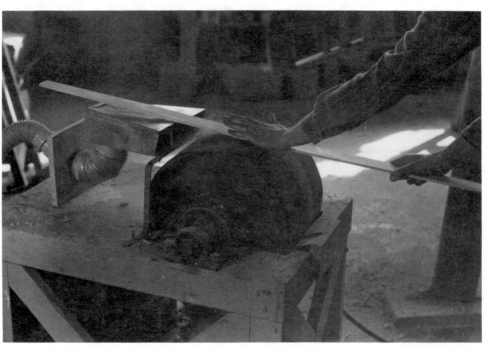

Shaping the edges of the rib stock with a molding head on a radial arm saw. (P.H. DesLauriers)

required to get good results in contouring the corner of the taper, but it becomes second nature as the job progresses.

Virtually the same type of setup can be achieved by securing a hand-held router upside down under a working surface fitted with a hole large enough to allow the bit to turn properly above the surface of the table. A temporary fence can then be added, approximating nicely the function of an expensive shaping unit. (See figure, Chapter 5.)

It is necessary to sand the newly shaped edges of the ribs—either lightly on a cushion-surfaced power unit such as the drum sander, or more diligently by hand—to achieve a finish comparable to that of the surface of the rib. Label the finished ribs according to length and mark the center with a line on the back surface. For exact alignment, I usually make this mark ¾ inch from the exact center of the rib, so that if I align my mark precisely at the edge of the strongback when bending on, the actual center of the rib is exactly where it belongs. (See illustration, Chapter 8.)

Thwarts

The ash thwarts are cut from stock planed on both sides to ¾ inch thick. Trace the pattern onto the stock and carefully cut it out on the bandsaw; then smooth or fair the edges with a spokeshave or a rasp. Shape the thwarts with a radius bit on a

Detail of shaping on ribs.

Cutting a thwart out of ash stock on the bandsaw.

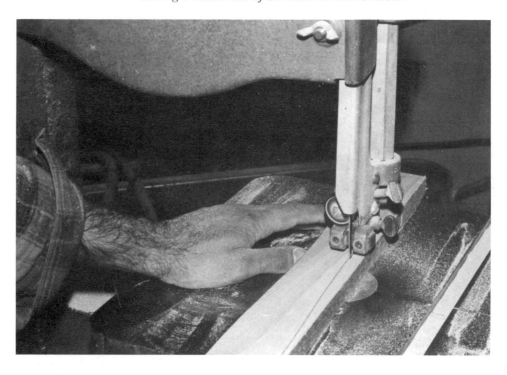

Fairing the edges of the thwart with a spokeshave prior to shaping them.

A hand-held router is used for shaping the edges of the thwarts.

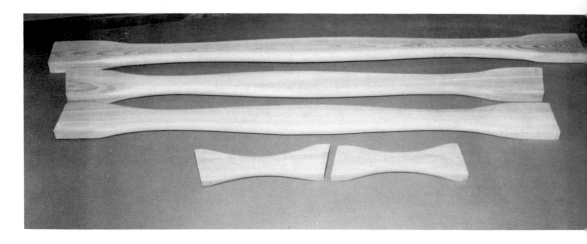

The finished thwarts ready for installation.

hand-held router, moving it along all four corners of the thwart, stopping a few inches from the end in each case. Then finish up the pieces handsomely either on the drum sander or by some alternate sanding method.

This canoe model has five thwarts—a center thwart 35¼ inches long, two quarter thwarts 30½ inches long, and two short tie-down thwarts only 8 inches long. In the case of a new design or an experimental model, it is wise to wait until the prototype is built and the ideal placement of the thwarts determined before taking pains to prepare thwarts that may never be used.

Seat stock for use with prewoven natural cane fillers measures ⅞ inch molded and 1⅜ inches sided. It should be planed smoothly on all surfaces, but the corners should be left square until after the pieces have been joined together.

Decks

The decks are cut from planed stock at least as thick as the molded dimension of the gunwale, in this case 1¹⁄₁₆ inches. If a slight crown or camber is going to be carved into the deck, additional thickness will be necessary. In this particular case I will use stock 1⅜ inches thick. The first step is tracing the pattern onto the stock and cutting out the decks on the bandsaw. Since the sides of this particular pattern are not perfectly straight (they have a mild curve designed into them), I will have to smooth the edges with a spokeshave, taking care to eliminate any high or hard spots that will prevent the deck from fitting snugly against the inside surface of the inwale. A block plane would serve as well on a deck with straight sides. The 18′6″ White guide canoe is straight-sided at the ends, so it is unnecessary to bevel the edges of the deck on this particular model.

Once the edges are smooth and fair, draw a line along each edge 1¹⁄₁₆ inches from the bottom surface. The ⁵⁄₁₆ inch above this line is the wood that is going to be shaped into the crown or camber. First work the corners away with a miniplane or

Cutting out the deck on the bandsaw.

Fairing the edge of the deck with a spokeshave to ensure a snug fit.

Carving a crown into the deck with a spokeshave.

spokeshave, and it is not long before a rough crown begins to materialize. Refine it with the cutting tools, and then a rasp, to achieve the desired crown. Then take the deck to the versatile drum sander for final shaping and sanding.

This completes the major milling portion of the operation, with the exception of a few accessories that will be covered later in the book. The shop is crowded with neat stacks of freshly sanded white wood, and the time has come to make the final preparations for the actual construction of the canoe.

A Word about Ping-Pong

"Them sports would ask for anything. One of them asked me to bring along a ping-pong table up river so his children could have some amusement out there in the wilderness. Jesus Christ. Well, I loaded that ping-pong table in a heavy crate aboard my 20-foot White and started poling upstream. It was heavy, let me tell you. It was likely the best goddamned championship ping-pong table you could buy in the world, because that's the kind this sport would have. When I got up to Leadbetter Falls it was pole up the falls or carry the damned table. I said I'm going to pole her up the falls by Jesus Christ.

"Couple of fellas there told me I couldn't do it. But I see a channel along the ledge and I poled into this channel. When the water backed up because the channel was stopped up with the canoe and me in it and the ping-pong table, when she backed up good enough, about as much as she was going to I give a shove, let me tell you, and kept on shoving until that canoe and freight was over the first pitch of the falls. I done that a couple times or more, plugging the channel and then shoving over the swell. I got cocky and she swung sideways and damned near went over, but I kept to her and shoved her straight again. It saved us lugging that god-damned ping-pong table over and around the falls."

Clarence Sands
in an interview with Lynn Franklin

7

Final Preparations

The builder must attend to a number of details several days before actually bending on the ribs. These include soaking, prebending, and shaping the stems and soaking and prebending the ends of gunwales. The ash stem stock bends readily with proper soaking and sufficient hot water or steam; the spruce rails will require very hot steam and a thorough soaking to be bent effectively. Presoaking both for a couple of days replaces some of the natural moisture that has been lost since the lumber was cut. A clear, running stream provides an ideal setup, but a pond will suffice, as will a tank of water in the shop or basement. Keeping the ends of the gunwales wrapped in wet rags and plastic on the shop floor may prove to be the best method of soaking these ungainly items.

Steaming

The capability of our particular unit to produce steam is limited. It works well enough for the cedar ribs, and when cranked up to maximum output, it will soften a spruce rail sufficiently to allow it to take a pretty good bend. However, it has proven barely adequate for the $\frac{7}{8}$-inch-thick stems, and the success ratio is much greater when they are boiled in a galvanized tank. We fill the tank with three or four inches of water and bring it to a boil. We boil the presoaked stem stock for at least an hour before taking out the first piece and testing it. If the test section appears sufficiently elastic, we attempt an actual bend.

Prebending

To do the prebending, the jig described in Chapter 5 is set on a bench or stool with the tip of the stem pointing down to the floor and the flat run of the stem parallel to

The stem stock is boiled in the galvanized tank.

the surface of the bench. One last look at the grain structure determines which surface will become the inside of the curve. The appropriate end of the stock is then placed beneath the bolt at the tip, and a wedge is driven between the bolt and the actual stem stock to hold it fast at this point. It is important to have the stem positioned properly, so that ample stock extends beyond the end of the jig. The opposite end of the wood is then grasped with protective gloves, and firmly and steadily the stick is bent tightly around the curve of the jig, stretching the wood as it is bent. When the bend is completed, another bolt is slid through the tabs at the remote end of the jig, over the stock; then another wedge is driven to hold this end fast. Our jig accommodates two such pieces (or enough stock for two canoes), and a second piece of stock is bent alongside the first before all the bolts and wedges are secured in place. The prebent stock should be allowed to set for at least 24 hours before being removed from the jig; otherwise the resilient wood will attempt to straighten itself out and lose some of its shape.

Although the mildly sweeping lines of the sheer of the White canoe do not require that the ends of the gunwales be prebent, I shall run through the procedure for the benefit of the builder who must deal with a more dramatic sheer line. Place the ends of the presoaked gunwales in the steam chamber as soon as appreciable steam begins to accumulate. It is important to put a few short test pieces in with the actual gunwales; it is a real catastrophe to snap a milled gunwale and not have a spare available. The wood will require considerable exposure to the steam for the grain to soften sufficiently; the temperature must be very hot and the moisture

Bending the boiled stem over the jig. Leather mittens protect the builder's hands.

The bent stem stock is in place, and wedges are driven to hold it tightly against the jig.

Prebending a gunwale over the jig and securing it with clamps.

The gunwales are clamped in place on the form in preparation for the rib bending.

level inside the chamber must be kept extremely high. When the test sections appear pliable, try a sample on the jig to see how easily it bends. If it bends readily, remove a gunwale from the chamber and, using a wooden chip for protection, clamp the end of it onto the crosspiece of the jig. Taking great care to prevent the rail from twisting, ply it slowly but steadily around the jig until the bend is complete. Clamp it firmly to several of the crosspieces to make sure that it doesn't twist as it dries. The jig should be wide enough to accommodate the ends of all four gunwales at one time.

We now encounter a procedural problem, because while one end of the gunwales is drying on the form, there is no effective way to steam the other end. To avoid a separate steaming, you can plan to finish this task at the same time that you bend the ribs. Suppose you bend one end of the gunwales the day before the rib-bending operation. After allowing the ends of the gunwales to set overnight, remove them from the jig and fire up the steamer. When sufficient steam has developed, stuff the straight ends into the chamber and allow them to soften. When they are adequately saturated, withdraw them, bend them temporarily over the jig, and place the first batch of ribs into the steam unit. While the ribs are being exposed to the steam, remove the inwales one at a time from the jig and clamp them directly onto the canoe form where they will soon be required. There will be enough curve already set into the gunwales and enough suppleness left to allow the nimble builder to work them onto the form while they still are partially wet.

Cutting the prebent stem to the proper width.

Shaping the Stems

The stems must be prepared further. After the bent stock has set at least overnight, remove it from the jig and rip it to the proper width by feeding the curved piece through the blade of the table saw. Take the two matching stems to their respective ends of the form and mark them precisely for length as well as for placement of the notches that must be cut into them to receive the ribs. Mark these notches along the "bottom" edge or face of the stem on the flat run. To make the cuts as accurate as possible, you can use an actual cross section of a rib to mark the shapes of the notches precisely. Accuracy is vital at this point; the notches must be large enough to accommodate the ribs, but not so large as to result in a sloppy fit (see figure).

After marking the notches, cut them carefully on the bandsaw, and finish them with a sharp chisel or a rasp. The corners of the notches, particularly those nearest the curve, should also be relieved with the rasp to provide a less angular shape for the ribs to bend over.

The curved part of the stems will now have to be beveled from the tip end all the way to the first notch. The amount of this bevel is determined by the shape of the canoe, specifically the average angle at which the planking intersects the vertical curved section of the stem. To determine the bevel angle, place the end of a bevel gauge across the face of the stem section of the form, perpendicular to an imaginary centerline running the length of the form, as illustrated on page 102. The angle at which the planking approaches the stem can then be measured with the blade of the instrument, the actual angle being the difference between the bevel as measured and 90 degrees. On the White canoe, this angle is a shallow 11 degrees, but on some models it could be as great as 16 or 18 degrees.

You can cut this bevel on the actual stem by hand with a spokeshave or block plane, but it saves a great deal of labor if you make the cuts on the bandsaw or the radial arm saw. I prefer the bandsaw for this task, but the blade must be in good, sharp condition to do the job accurately. Tilt the table of the bandsaw to the proper angle, and clamp a square-sided guide or fence to the surface; position it so that when the square stem is run through, a wedge-shaped slice of material is removed from the side closest to the blade. The blade should barely graze the top corner of the stock, leaving the uppermost or "inner" surface virtually the full sided dimension, while the bottom surface (or stem face) is substantially reduced to achieve the proper bevel. Introduce the tip of the curved stem to the blade, and slowly feed the stem to the saw, taking pains to keep the stem face flush with the table surface at the blade. Make the cut to within two inches of the first notch, then slowly lift the stem face from the surface as you continue to push the stem through the saw. By the time the blade is abreast the middle of the notch, the stem should be lifted clear of the blade, resulting in a gradual diminishing of the bevel until it actually disappears at this point (see illustration).

Bevel the second stem on one side in the same manner, and then change the setup to bevel the second side as follows: Replace the square-sided guide with one that has been appropriately beveled. Position this beveled guide so that the previously beveled side of the stem rests against the angled side and the blade slices a matching bevel on the square side of the stem. To accomplish this, the table must be tilted in the opposite direction, but the angle is kept the same.

Cutting a notch in the stem to accommodate a rib. (P.H. DesLauriers)

Using a chisel to shape precisely the notches in the stems.

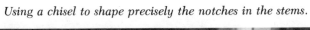

Using a rasp to relieve the sharp corners of the notches, thus allowing the ribs to bend more evenly.

Using a bevel gauge to determine the bevel of the stem.

Cutting the bevel on the stem with a bandsaw. Note tilt of table and wooden guide. (P.H. DesLauriers)

At the end of the cut, the stem is gradually lifted from the table, diminishing the bevel until it runs out. (P.H. DesLauriers)

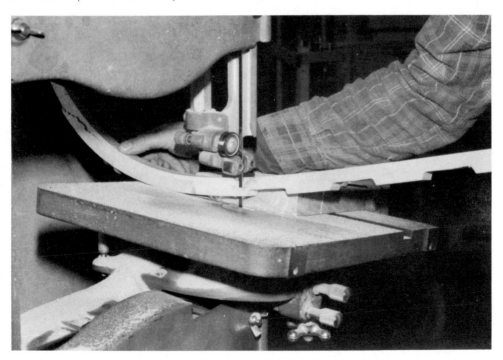

Using a spokeshave to smooth the bevel cut on the bandsaw.

The beveled sides, which may be a little rough at this point, can be sanded accurately with a sanding disk fitted to the table saw and tilted to the proper angle. The remainder of the stem, particularly those sections that will be visible within the finished canoe, should be sanded smooth either by hand or on the drum sander. They are then ready to be attached to the building form in readiness for the frame bending.

Making a Strongback

At this point you should prepare a strongback to hold the ribs flush with the form at the centerline as they are bent. A standard 2 x 4 timber long enough to reach from stem to stem serves nicely. Drill holes through the molded dimension of this member, corresponding to the tapped threaded sockets located on the building form for this purpose. Place 5″ x ½″ bolts through the strongback and thread them into the sockets, holding the 2 x 4 snugly against three ⁵⁄₁₆-inch-thick spacers. The resulting space between the form and the strongback can be adjusted by tightening or loosening these bolts during the bending process. Ideally the straight ribs will have to be coaxed to get them to pass between the form and the strongback, which will then hold them effectively in the proper position along the centerline at each of the steel bands. Once the strongback is in position on the form, the rib lengths are marked on it at each position, providing a convenient visual guide for determining exact rib placement, which will eliminate a lot of trial-and-error fumbling during the bending process.

With these details out of the way, there is nothing to prevent the builder from embarking on what should be one of the most enjoyable and satisfying steps of the entire construction, bending the cedar frames, which will complete the skeleton of the canoe.

Soaking the Stems

February thaws are welcome anywhere, but in Washington County (Maine) they are a particular blessing. This one had pretty much dissolved the snow except deep in the woods, and the little stream behind the shop, normally restrained by layers of thick ice that time of the year, was a tea-colored, boiling torrent tripping over its own haystacks on its way to the ice-choked inlet below.

Never one to miss an opportunity, Rollin capitalized on this unusual situation by carrying a sheaf of stem stock down to the brook and securing it to a clump of alder, for the normal day or two presoaking. That night the wind struck up from the northwest, ruthlessly driving the balmy, moist system we had so enjoyed far out into the Atlantic and sending the mercury plummeting to the far side of the zero mark.

It was two days later that we decided to boil up the stems in order to bend them over the forms. Rollin returned to the shop empty-handed, with frosted whiskers and a blank expression on his face, grabbed the axe, and, without a word, trudged back out into the numbing wind.

Twenty minutes of chopping was about all he needed to liberate the stock from its prison of solid brown ice. I don't recall whether or not the freezing technique was as effective as the normal soaking procedure.

8

Bending On
and Fairing the Ribs

The builder has already accomplished at least one steam-bending exercise by the time he has reached this point, so the apprehension that normally inhibits the amateur from attempting a woodworking project that entails steam-bending has by now been dissolved. Further encouragement should come from the fact that bending the cedar ribs is actually much easier than bending either the stem stock or the gunwales.

All that is required is a methodical approach to the problem. If the appropriate preparations are completed, and a logical attack plan mentally ironed out, the actual rib bending should be a smooth and enjoyable operation. The builder and his helper will have to work rapidly, but not hurriedly. The ribs remain pliable long enough to secure them over the form before a panic situation develops.

The steam box itself has already been discussed. It need not be elaborate, but it should be large enough to accommodate at least half the ribs in such a way that most of their surface area is exposed to the steam. The heat source, whether wood, propane, or oil, must be sufficient to generate a good quantity of steam throughout the exercise, and the boiler or kettle must be capable of holding enough water to last through the entire operation. If the boiler should run low during the job, it is possible to add enough hot water to finish up, pausing long enough to allow the added water to begin producing adequate steam. The final caution is not to allow the ribs to be exposed to the steam for too long. There is a critical point in the steam-softening of wood after which the process actually begins to dry the wood out, making it extremely brittle. If the bending begins as soon as the first ribs become elastic enough to take the curves, and if the work proceeds steadily, however, there should be little danger of this occurring.

The first step is to fire up the boiler. The ribs have been prepared, marked, and sorted. It will prove helpful to place these ribs into the steam box in some logical

108

order, based on the fact that the actual bending sequence will proceed from the middle of the canoe toward one end and then from the middle to the remaining end. Place the ribs in the chamber as soon as sufficient steam develops, dipping each frame in water just before putting it into the box. Wetting the ribs seems to increase their capacity to absorb the steam, but it is not advisable to soak them in water overnight, as was done with the stem stock, because the wood will swell and raise the grain, virtually negating all the presanding work. The steaming itself will cause the grain to rise a bit too, but the finish sanding inside the canoe will still be minimal compared to what would be required if the ribs had not been presanded at all.

The form itself is set bottom up on a pair of sawhorses, with the strongback bolted into place and the stems secured in their respective slots with either wire or twine. The inner gunwales are clamped to the recessed backup strip running along the sheer line of the form as in the illustration. Take care that the rails are positioned properly, right side up, with the beveled side facing outboard ready to receive the ribs.

Assemble the hammers, nails, a tack puller, an electric drill with a $\frac{3}{32}$-inch bit and a wrench for adjusting the tension on the strongback. Lay them out in readiness on the canoe form.

Bending On

After 45 minutes of exposure to the steam, the ribs are probably ready to bend. Pull one from the box and test its suppleness. If it seems adequately pliable, take it to the midship position on the form and slide it face down under the strongback until the mark on the back aligns with the edge of the strongback itself. Now the reason for marking the rib $\frac{3}{4}$ inch from the actual center becomes apparent. If the rib passes too easily under the strongback, it will be necessary to tighten the nearest bolt enough to ensure that the rib is held firmly down on the metal band. The builder and his helper work on opposite sides of the form. Each places one hand firmly on the back surface of the rib adjacent to the strongback, on what will be the bottom of the canoe. With the other hand, each person stretches the rib tightly around the contour, following the metal band exactly. It is mandatory that both edges of the rib lie flush on the band, but this is a greater consideration in the quarters of the canoe than here at the midship position.

When the rib is in position, it is held against the outboard surface of the gunwale with the extra length projecting beyond the rail on either side and nailed in place with $\frac{3}{4}$-inch bronze boat nails or galvanized ring or box nails. Drive two nails beside one another at about the vertical center of the gunwale. From this point, simply proceed one rib at a time toward one end of the canoe. The proper tension of the strongback must be maintained as the work proceeds.

The taper that has been cut on one side of the rib should face amidships rather than toward one end of the canoe. The metal bands near the ends of the canoe, and consequently also the ribs, have a definite slant or cant to them. The function of this cant is to allow the ribs to sit flush even as the girth of the canoe is diminishing rapidly, resulting in some rather complex contours. When the taper is faced amid-

The strongback is in position on the form, ready for the cedar ribs.

Pulling a steam-softened rib from the steam box.

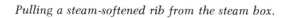

Working as a team, two people can frame out a canoe in a bit more than an hour.

Good bending technique: The rib is held in place firmly and stretched as it is bent.

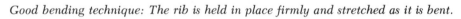

ships, it has the effect of neutralizing this cant to some extent, giving the ribs in the finished canoe a more vertical appearance.

The ends of the strongback should not project over the stems, even though you must bend on several ribs at the very end of the canoe. Instead, hold the centers of these ribs firmly in the prepared notches in the stem with the heel of your palm, and bend and fasten the ribs to the gunwales. Next, drill two holes through the ribs and into the stem, and drive in the bronze ring nails to hold the ribs solidly in place within the notches. The majority of rib casualties will take place in this vicinity because of the extraordinarily sharp bends required. Still, with proper steaming, no more than two or three should break at each end, and only the rare one will snap elsewhere on the canoe.

When the builders reach the end, they start once again amidships and proceed in like manner to the other end. When all the ribs are bent, they should be allowed to sit overnight before fairing. Some builders bend the narrow half-ribs onto the form at this time. As explained in Chapter 10, these small structural members add strength to the oft-abused bottom of the canoe and form a platform for keeping duffel off the planking between the ribs. In practice I have found it difficult to keep the half-ribs straight and in their exact positions through the planking process, and I secure them into the hull after it is built instead, with much neater, more satisfactory results.

There are several distinct steps in the construction of a canoe that, when completed, inspire a deep feeling of exuberance and fulfillment in the heart of the builder, be he amateur or professional. For me, the pattern of the light ribs bent evenly around the graceful contours of the darker form is a sight that warms me to the core, refreshes my spirit, and admittedly inflates my ego a bit as well. The key to the whole wonderfully simple system—the backbone of a craft that will carry its master through surging rapids, across wind-tossed lakes, and down glassy thoroughfares alike—is laid out in bent wood before the builder's eyes. It has been put together with his own hands, following centuries-old principles. No matter how many canoes I may build in my lifetime, I shall each time pause and step back to admire fully this superbly functional sculpture and the ancient technology from which it has evolved.

Fairing

Like many other individually hand-crafted objects, the hull frame, however fine, may be a bit less than perfect at this stage. Careful examination, or better yet, actual physical testing with a section of planking, may reveal that a few ribs are slightly out of position or that despite the great care that was taken during the bending operation, a few edges are not quite flush with the metal bands. This situation could be caused by a slight, even undetectable, unfair spot on the form, especially if it is an old one that has been used extensively and moved around considerably. If they are serious enough, these uneven spots could potentially cause unfair hollows or bulges in the hull of the canoe, or at the very least result in gaps along the edges of the ribs where the planking is not lying perfectly flush against them as it should.

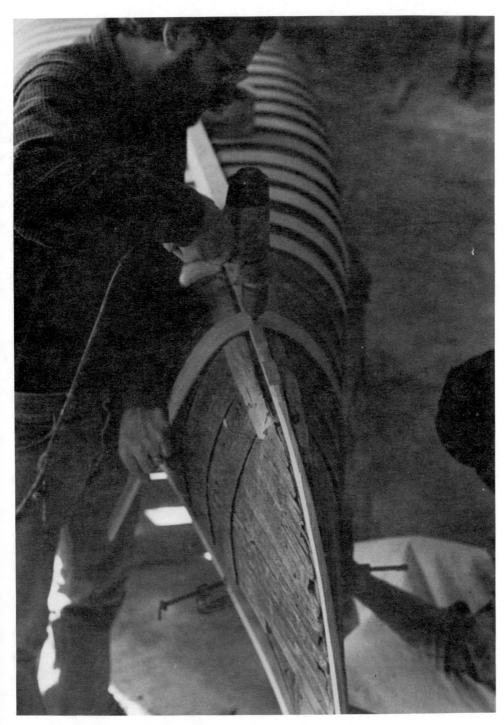

Predrilling a small hole in the ash stem before securing the rib with bronze nails.

The supple ribs are bent around the notches in the stem.

The half-ribs may be bent onto the form and secured as soon as a few planks are laid down, or they may be put in after the hull is completed, as described later.

It's likely that the situation isn't serious, but since it can be remedied easily, it is worthwhile to go over the entire canoe, locate any trouble areas, however minor, and eliminate them. It will be well worth the effort in terms of the final product.

Most of the trouble spots, if any, will be near the very ends of the canoe, because the metal bands and the steam-saturated ribs may conform differently to the contoured surface. If you take a section of planking long enough to span five or six frames, place it across the ribs, and move it up and down along the surfaces, any problem that prevents the planking from lying flush becomes immediately apparent. Generally, it is simply a raised edge that causes the planking to approach the adjacent ribs at a slight angle. If the wedge-shaped gap caused by the offending frame is substantial, the end of the culprit may actually have to be repositioned slightly along the gunwale. Removing the nails and moving the end ahead or back even a small fraction of an inch can usually bring the renegade into line.

If the gap is very minor, the problem will be eliminated when the entire surface of the skeleton is attacked with the fairing block described in Chapter 5. This instrument is applied in two directions along the whole canoe, to eliminate any minute inconsistencies in the fairness of the hull, before the planking is applied. The block itself is 16 inches long and surfaced with 40-grit floor-sanding paper. Hold it firmly to the back surface of the ribs with both hands and move it horizontally along the hull, fairing six or eight ribs at a stroke, one section of the canoe at a time. The ends of the blocks are curved upward to prevent the block from catching the edges of the ribs and moving them out of place, but it is still necessary to make

The ribs bent in place.

Checking for fairness with a section of planking stock. Any rib out of line will show up as a gap between planking and ribs.

sure that the centers of the ribs are held fast by the strongback. If tightening the bolts is not sufficient to accomplish this, the long, thin wedges that were cut from the rib stock to form the tapers are ideal for driving under the strongback at each rib to bind them more securely in the proper position.

The horizontal strokes of the fairing block will result in obvious linear scratches across the backs of the ribs. These marks provide an additional indication of the fairness of the hull skeleton. If the backs of the ribs form a perfectly fair surface, the scratches will extend uniformly across the entire width of each rib. If the surface is unfair, some sections of the ribs will not be affected by the sanding, and these will become obvious. Usually a few more strokes will bring these into alignment, but should this prove insufficient, you may have to reposition the rib slightly rather than risk removing too much material. The actual material removed by this fairing should in fact be minimal—normally too little to be measured. The strength, if any, lost as a result of this sanding is more than compensated for by the increased integral strength of the unit, with all the planking resting smoothly on the ribs.

When you have completed the horizontal fairing in one section, use a vertical treatment with the same block to further smooth the surface. Repeat this two-step process at each section of the hull, taking care each time to overlap the previous section by one or two ribs. The resulting rib framework should be perfectly fair and smooth, and a section of planking placed across it horizontally at any location should sit evenly across the back surfaces of all the ribs that it touches.

Applying the fairing block to ensure a smooth surface for the planking.

The tacked strips of wood hold the ribs in place while the center is faired and the chalkline is struck.

Ready for planking, the ribs have been faired, the chalkline struck, and the strongback braced to one side of the centerline.

When the fairing process is completed, tack long, thin strips of wood longitudinally across the ribs the entire length of the canoe. These keep the ribs in position when the strongback is removed to facilitate fairing the area in its immediate proximity. When the area along the centerline is faired to the rest of the canoe, run a chalkline from the middle of one stem to the middle of the other and strike a centerline the length of the canoe as a visual reference for the proper placement of the garboard or center planks. Then place the strongback just to one side of the centerline, braced from the overhead with upright supports, and secure the ribs in position once again with wedges driven under the strongback in preparation for laying the first garboard.

Beaching a Canoe

"We didn't have motors then, of course, and we went out.
The seas were so big around me I couldn't see over them and I
dodged all the breakers until I got across to the beach. Out in
about six feet of water the big ones were breaking clear to the
bottom. By golly, I missed all the big ones and I intended to
get in on the beach far enough with my freight and with
Treadwell to put it ashore dry. But just as I got onto the edge
of the beach one of them big breakers broke right over the
canoe and knocked the canoe and us straight down to the bottom. Treadwell threw his hands up in the air and said,
'What are we gonna do?'

"I said, 'Just hold your breath for about three minutes and
the next one will take us right in onto the beach!"

Myron Smart
in an interview with Lynn Franklin

9

Planking the Hull

Planking the canoe is a meticulous but straightforward process. The milled planking is pliable enough to conform to the contours of much of the hull with very little shaping.

Laying Out the Pattern

It is helpful to determine a planking pattern for the canoe before actually beginning this step. The builder must develop a system for his canoe whereby he can compensate for the great difference in girth between the center section and the quarters of the canoe in a visually acceptable way. Although the planking pattern may not seem readily visible between the ribs in the interior of the craft, a haphazard, piecemeal arrangement will detract from the overall symmetry of the canoe. The pattern can be determined on the canoe itself, or on the lines plan if this is available. The illustration shows how the girth difference can be resolved mathematically on the body plan on the drafting board or on the mold loft floor. The weakness of this system is that it really doesn't afford the builder a graphic, three-dimensional representation of the resulting pattern as would an accurate perspective drawing of the canoe.

Therefore, it's best for the novice to lay out his pattern directly on the backs of the bent ribs by means of a supple 1″ x ¼″ batten long enough to span a bit over half the length of the canoe. Since most canoes are symmetrical, it is necessary to do this on only one-quarter of the actual canoe to derive the entire pattern. To begin, mark on every third rib the width of the planking (in this case, 3 inches) from the chalk centerline, starting at a point one station beyond the midship section and ending at the point where the actual curve of the stem begins. Then tack the batten so its outside edge just touches these marks and draw a line along it. Allow the end

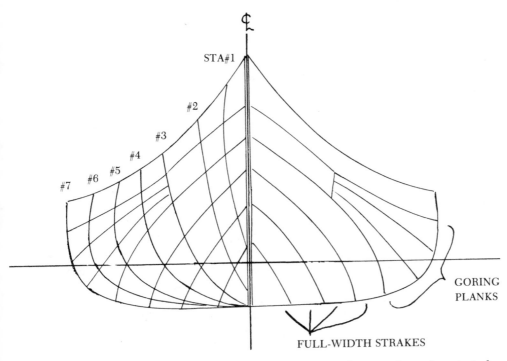

Determining a goring plan on a hypothetical body plan. In this case, it works out nicely, tapering strakes 5, 6, and 7 from full width at station 7 to one-third width or one inch at station 3.

A better method of determining a visually acceptable planking pattern is to use a batten to draw out the full-width strakes on the backs of the bent ribs, thus leaving exactly the area left to be "gored."

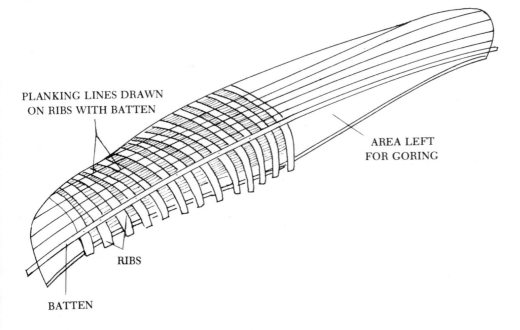

of the batten to run by the curve of the stem naturally and draw the line according-ly. The resulting line on the ribs represents the lay of the garboard plank, which has a great deal of twist in it at the ends.

The principal difference between planking a canoe and planking a typical wooden boat is the fact that the ⁵⁄₃₂-inch canoe planking can be made to conform to much of the hull without any tapering or shaping. As a result, the first four or five planks on each side of the canoe are secured virtually full width, whereas on a larger boat with thicker planking, this timesaving procedure is impossible, and each plank from the garboard on up has its own peculiar shape.

Normally the straight, full-width planks can be run all the way from the centerline out to the actual turn of the bilge at the midship station. This will en-compass anywhere from four 3-inch-wide planks, including the garboard, on a small round-bottomed craft to as many as seven on a large flat-bottomed 20-foot guide canoe. On the 18′6″ White guide canoe, five full-width planks per side can be put on before the builder must compensate for the changing girth.

The builder will mark his hull off accordingly. When these strakes have been determined, the distance remaining to the sheer should be measured amidships and at the narrowest point in the quarter of the canoe, before the sheer starts to rise sharply. On a typical 18-foot canoe, these distances might be 12 inches amidships and 6 inches at the point seven ribs from the end, resulting in a difference in girth between these two points of just 6 inches. This difference can be resolved by taper-ing two planks from their full width amidships to a fine point on rib number seven. However, a feather edge is not particularly desirable in any boatbuilding exercise, because it has little strength and tends to be easily split by fastenings. Therefore, a better solution would be to taper three planks from full width amidships to one inch at rib number seven. In this method the ends of the three tapered strakes form a joint with the shorter plank at the end. The difficulty in forming the full-width planks around the bilge has also been relieved by using the much more easily handled tapered (or gored) strakes.

In practice, the actual dimensions seldom work out this handily because of the limitations of the uniform plank width and the constantly changing shape of the sheer line. Even in this ideal case, small sections near the rise of the sheer will have to be filled in by short, rather irregular sections of plank. This practice is con-sidered acceptable in canoe construction because these wedge-shaped sections, ly-ing as they do along the gunwales, have a minimal effect on the strength of the hull and are not at all obvious from inside the canoe.

Planking

Having arrived at a plan for placing the planks on the hull, it is time to gather the planking tools and put the theory into actual practice. At the top of the list are the tacks and tack hammer, a block or a model-making miniplane, the linoleum or utility knife, a small hardwood block to use as a straightedge when cutting the planking, and a combination square for marking the butt joints. A tack puller, the smallest bronze or galvanized nails available (see Chapter 4), a drill with a ³⁄₃₂-inch or ⁷⁄₆₄-inch bit, a vessel of hot water, and some rags wrapped around a stick for sloshing the water onto the planking can also be considered essential.

Cutting the planking. The knife is held at a 45-degree angle to form the beveled butt joint.

In planking the canoe, the builder must start with one of the garboard strakes, which represent the most difficult challenge of the entire planking operation. The garboard must twist nearly 90 degrees from its flat horizontal position at the bottom of the canoe amidships to a nearly vertical attitude along the stem. Along the flat of the stem the garboard must flex or cup itself sharply to accommodate the two opposing situations. This sounds like a pretty stiff order to fill, but it is not at all impossible for a properly selected, well-soaked cedar plank. This is one situation where straight grain is beneficial. Again, however, wood with grain lines that are too close together has little chance of flexing enough to perform the task without cracking.

The entire garboard strake should be laid out at this point, whether it is to be a single long strake or one made up of shorter sections. In the latter case, determine at which ribs butt joints will be made. Execute the joints themselves by first drawing perpendicular lines across the ends of the two abutting planks; then, with the hardwood block as a guide, use a sharp linoleum knife to score several passes across the plank. Hold the knife at a 45-degree angle to the surface of the canoe, protecting it by using a section of ¾-inch pine as a cutting surface. Generally two passes are adequate to complete the neatly beveled cut. Fit the end of the abutting plank with a complementary angle that fits tightly over the first bevel, resulting in a strong, tight, overlapped joint located in the center of the 2⅜-inch-wide rib.

In fastening the garboard, begin in the middle of the canoe and work toward one of the ends, laying the edge of the plank precisely along the chalkline down the center of the canoe. Place the tacks in a three-point pattern as illustrated, alter-

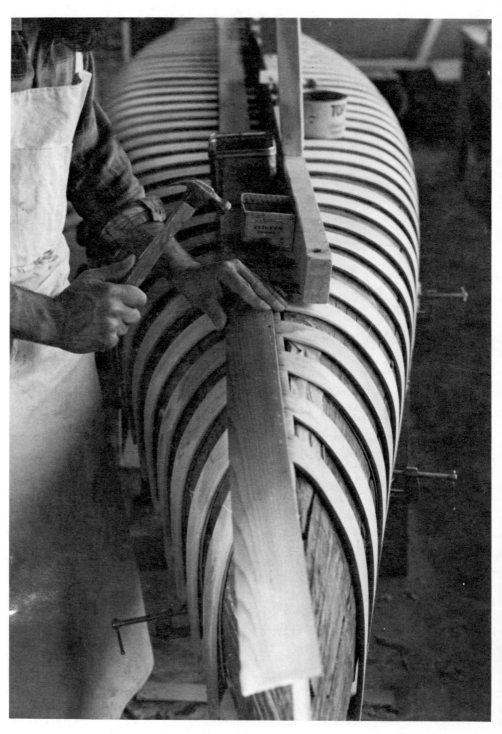

Fastening the garboard to the stem with bronze nails.

Hot water is applied to the garboard to soften the fibers.

nating direction on each strake. The tacks, which are driven soundly but not brutally, should be spaced to take maximum advantage of the width of the rib without breaking through the shaped edge of the rib itself. Fasten three tacks along the butt line itself on each of the two planks, and drive two additional tacks into each plank at the far edge of the rib to secure the joint further. The outside tacks must be driven very close to the edge of the planking. To prevent the planking from being split by the fastenings, drill $\frac{1}{16}$-inch holes through the planking or reinforce the edge with a hand-held hardwood push stick.

As the builder approaches the stem, it becomes necessary to soak the back of the garboard plank with very hot water. This method of softening the grain is simpler than actually steaming the garboard, and it works just as well. The edge of the planking is fastened with $\frac{5}{8}$-inch bronze ring nails or similar galvanized nails along the centerline of the stem, between the rib notches (after predrilling holes), and allowed to run by the start of the curve of the stem. After repeatedly soaking the plank, bend it down gently until the unfastened edge lies along the vertical ribs; then fasten it. Working slowly and cautiously toward the ends, adding hot water periodically, is the only method of completing this task without splitting the plank. Once the edge is secured to the last rib, the worry is over. Fasten the end of the plank with the same nails to the curve of the stem after drilling, and trim the rest of the plank with the linoleum knife to conform with the curve. Then fasten the shaped edge to the stem with an additional three or four nails (see figure). Work the opposite end of the garboard into position in a similar manner.

The garboard is bent slowly down until it sits flush on the ribs.

The end of the garboard is nailed to the stem.

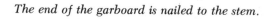

Finally the garboard is trimmed close to the stem and the fastening is completed.

The next few strakes are relatively easy to attach. Again it is advisable to lay out the full strake whether it is one long plank or several sections. Any butts should fall at least four ribs away from those of the garboard. Once again, proceed from the center section toward the ends. Hold the plank firmly against the edge of the garboard and fasten it in the same manner. Once again, apply hot water in the quarters to get the plank to twist sufficiently. Use the hardwood push stick to prevent the edge of the plank from splitting.

Normally the end of the second plank will fit tightly against the edge of the garboard without much applied force or "edge-set." Sometimes, however, the edge of the plank overlaps the garboard when allowed to assume its natural course. The opposite situation occurs wherever a wedge-shaped gap remains between the two strakes, despite a fair amount of edge-setting. The plank should not be fastened any closer than a dozen ribs from the end before the developing situation there is checked to allow enough leeway for appropriate action. In the former case the builder can get the plank to fit properly by using his modeling plane to shave the end of the plank sufficiently. The opposite condition usually occurs when material farther up the strake prevents the end from fitting snugly. This trouble spot can be located by allowing the plank to overlap the garboard in the quarters of the canoe until the end fits properly. This overlapping material is then removed carefully with the plane, and the plank is set firmly into position. The builder should be aware that too much edge-set can introduce appreciable tension into the plank, a condition that can bulge the edges of the plank or even loosen the fastenings so that

A few strakes attached. A hardwood wedge is again used to prevent minor splits.

Detail of the nailing pattern in the quarter of the canoe.

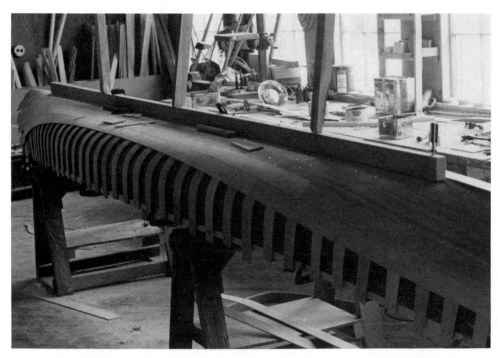

With the full-width strakes in place, it is easy to see the area to be gored.

wide seams later develop between the planks. To facilitate removing the canoe from the form, the ends of the second and all succeeding planks are allowed to run past the stem without being fastened.

The tapered or gored planks present the second real challenge in the planking operation. The taper is not a straight line running from the full width of the plank to the one-inch width at the narrow end, but rather a gentle convex curve beginning a few ribs beyond the center and extending to the tip of the small end. Therefore, simply striking a line along a plank and precutting the taper on the power saw is not possible. Practiced canoe builders simply attach the full-width plank to the center of the canoe and, using the linoleum knife and plane, fit the plank by eye as they go, achieving a snug fit without any measuring, precutting, or seemingly undue attention. The amateur builder will probably be more comfortable—not to mention successful—if he has a visual mark to which to work. He can use a batten to mark off the shape of the planks (which may already have been done to arrive at the planking pattern) and transfer the various widths at each of the ribs to corresponding points on the plank. A fair curve can be run through these points with a light batten, and the taper can be precut on the bandsaw or even with the linoleum knife. The precut plank can then be fastened at the midship station and finely fit with a plane as it is fastened. A fair amount of hot water will be required to coax these strakes around the bilge, and excessive edge-setting here will result in severe bulges between the ribs.

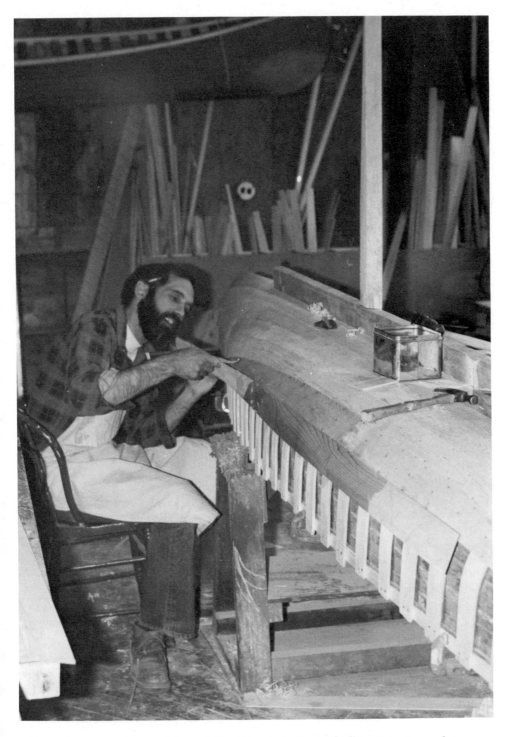

Beginning a gore by attaching a full-width plank, then whittling it to its rough taper.

The three gored planks join with a single plank in a narrow part of the canoe.

Bevel the three tapered ends as one to form a butt joint with a single strake at each end of the canoe. It may be possible to fit one more additional strake, if there is one, before moving to the other side. Generally, however, it is easier to fit the sheer strake after the canoe is taken off the form. Move the strongback over onto the first garboard, and plank the other side of the hull in the same manner.

When this is finished, it is the builder's great privilege to remove his handiwork from the form and get his first memorable look at the soft, elegant symmetry of the interior of the canoe—a vision he is not likely to forget soon. To accomplish this, he removes the strongback and pulls the gunwales free of their imprisoning slots one section at a time. If this proves difficult, the builder can usually release the grip without damaging the gunwale by pressing down on the actual bottom of the canoe and pulling outward at the same time. The hull is then freed with someone at each end lifting the open-ended, basketlike structure gingerly from the form, exposing to all the world the skill and care imparted by the builder into the construction of the hull.

The mini smoothing plane is used to fit the tapered plank.

All planked up! The very ends of the planking have not yet been secured to the stem.

Removing the canoe from the form by pressing down on the hull and pulling the rail free from its slot.

The ends are opened slightly and the hull is lifted slowly.

The basic hull—here the builder gets his first look at the canoe's interior.

Full Circle

It is important to focus effort on preserving the basic wood canoe, for it represents the simplest, most flexible, purest form of an efficient and graceful watercraft. It has gone full circle from enjoying a golden age to being largely neglected to being rediscovered with widespread popularity. That it remains basically unchanged speaks for its intrinsic value. With this in mind a good canoe builder wants to concentrate with no little effort on selecting materials with integrity, on paying attention to detail, and working with pride of craftsmanship.

Clint Tuttle

10

Completing the Hull, Clinching, and Sanding

The hull at this stage still has a way to go before being considered complete. It is an almost fluid unit and can be influenced to take a variety of forms by changing the shape of the decks or the placement of the thwarts, which ultimately lock the hull into its more rigid condition. The builder must continue his careful attention so that the hull will be straight and properly proportioned.

Positioning Spacers

Shape is first introduced into the structure by placing specially prepared spacers at strategic locations. These are nothing more than pieces of wood notched at the proper width to fit over the gunwales and hold a section of the canoe at its proper beam, much as the thwarts will do later. Generally, one such spacer is set amidships, with an additional one at each quarter, close enough to the ends to bring the separated gunwales nearly together at the ends, but not so close as to eliminate all horizontal movement of the two gunwales in relation to one another. Once this is accomplished, the builder has his first clue to the true shape of the finished canoe.

Joining Deck, Gunwales, and Stem

The next task is to bind the diverse elements of the end of the canoe into a solid, neat, and straight unit. On the surface, this does not seem difficult, but it will challenge the builder's ingenuity as well as his ability to work carefully. There are all too many carelessly built craft in use, their stems not perfectly straight vertically (although probably their owners have never noticed). This problem can be avoided entirely by proper attention to a few principles at this stage of construction.

The gunwales, decks, and stems and their ultimate union control the character of the very ends of the canoe. The planking merely reinforces this relationship. The

143

Ready for completion, the fluid hull awaits further attention.

relative horizontal positions of the two gunwales determine whether all these members are in proper alignment with the rest of the canoe. The vertical attitude of the stem must be precisely 90 degrees to the plane of the bottom of the canoe.

There are several acceptable methods of joining the deck to the stem. The simplest is illustrated in the figure. In this method, the point of the deck is cut off flush with the back of the stem at a slight bevel to match the angle of the stem top. The deck and gunwales are aligned and joined (explained in detail later); they lock the stem into the triangular space formed by the gunwales and the end of the deck. A screw is angled through the stem up into the deck to secure the joint further. The whole joint is usually covered by a brass cap, which protects the end from excessive wear.

A much sounder method is a mortise-and-tenon-type joint, which is cut into the pieces before the decks are attached to the rails. To use this method, the builder first determines the exact height of the stem and its relationship to either of the two gunwales by lifting the gunwales up along the stem as high as they will go and pulling the stem tip back to its proper position. The top and bottom of the gunwales are then marked on the overly long stem, and the back surface of the stem is marked on each of the gunwales. The stem is then cut to length. The exact shape of the pointed end of the deck is centered and drawn on the resulting top surface of the stem. A wedge-shaped tenon is cut by backsaw and chisel, extending from the stem top down to the marks representing the bottom edge of the gunwales as in the illustration. The top half of the tenon is cut off, resulting in a tenon half as long as the thickness of the deck. The builder then cuts a complementary mortise into the

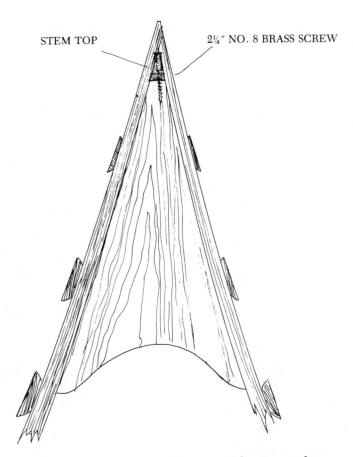

STEM TOP   2¼″ NO. 8 BRASS SCREW

*A simple joint at the deck is formed by running the stem up along
the deck, which has been nibbed off square. A wood screw provides the main strength in this method, along with the holding
power of the planking.*

deck, making sure the back surface is cut at an angle corresponding to the actual
run of the stem.

Whichever method you choose, it is necessary to saturate all parts liberally with
a good wood preservative before finally joining everything together. This is the one
area of the canoe most susceptible to dry rot because of its water-trapping con-
figuration.

After these cuts are made, position the deck properly and fasten it to the marked
gunwale. Cut the tip end of this gunwale at an angle matching the run of the opposite side of the deck so that the second gunwale will pass right alongside it,
making a neat joint beyond the deck tip.

To align the canoe, run a string from the inboard end of the farthest stem to the
tip of the deck being fastened. Determine the exact center of the midship spacer
and mark it as well as the center of the wide, curved end of the deck. The builder
achieves the proper alignment of the canoe visually by bringing the string into
exact alignment with the centerline of the canoe (as represented by the garboard

The two gunwales form a neat joint beyond the tip of the deck.

Aligning the stems. The string is used as a visual guide to ensure a straight canoe.

The clinched bronze nails ensure that the stem is locked securely in position.

seam) and the marked center points on the spacer and on the wide end of the deck. This is done by holding the unfastened gunwale alongside the deck and moving it back and forth horizontally in relation to the deck and the secured gunwale, while sighting down the string with one eye. The stem itself at this point is free, off to one side of the deck out of the way. At one particular position, all these reference points should be in a direct line. At this exact position, the builder marks the very back of the deck on the free gunwale. Sometimes, because of the considerable force required to hold the gunwale alongside the deck, it is beneficial to employ a "Spanish windlass" to bring the gunwales together for the alignment process.

With the gunwale marked for proper placement of the deck, hold the stem in its proper position and secure the free gunwale to the deck. The actual fastening should be done with 1½-inch No. 10 bronze or brass screws, three to a side on a short deck (under 12 inches long), and four for a longer one. Apply marine bedding compound to both edges of the deck before securing. The two inwales are fastened together beyond the tip of the deck by drilling a pair of ¹⁄₁₆-inch holes and securing them with clinched tacks. The stem, secure in its little enclosed niche, needs no further fastening, because the planking will help hold it fast when the ends are attached to the stem itself. Align the other end of the canoe and secure it similarly.

The ends of the planking, until now allowed to run free past the stem, are next fastened from the garboard on up the stem. Five-eighths-inch bronze ring nails are ideal for this, but similar galvanized fastenings will do. Predrilling the holes into the hard ash stem prevents the fastenings from being bent in the process and avoids

The ends of the planking are nailed to the stem. The crown of the deck is apparent here.

The cant ribs. The ends are cut to fit the ends of the canoe and thinned to wedge between stem and planking.

the possibility of splitting the planking. Three nails are sufficient to hold each plank in place, and a clinching iron or similar metal tool is held along the opposite side of the stem to support it as the nails are driven. When one side is completely fastened, the planking is trimmed flush with the stem face with the linoleum knife, and the other side is secured.

Installing Cant Ribs

The planking between the last bent ribs and the stems is unsupported by any frames, due to the inability of the ribs to take the tight bend during steaming. This distance is too great for the planks to span in such a vulnerable area, and the ends are generally strengthened by false or "cant" ribs. Cant ribs derive their name from the obvious slant they assume to match the last of the actual bent ribs. Usually they are not as thick as the standard ribs. The 18-foot White canoe requires two such frames in each end; the first is $\frac{7}{32}$ inch thick, and the second only $\frac{5}{32}$ inch. They are spaced in the same manner as the conventional ribs.

The bottom ends of the cant ribs are cut at an angle corresponding to the curve of the stem at the point where they will be situated. The cut is then sanded on the drum sander to almost a feather edge so that it may be set down between the stem and the secured planking. Properly fitted and positioned, the cant ribs will be difficult to distinguish from the actual ribs, and no novice would suspect that they were not actually bent around the stem.

Soaking the ends of the cant ribs prior to installing them.

The builder allows the ends of the cant ribs to soak in hot water for 15 minutes before they are secured; then he fastens them in their proper positions by holding them in place with a clinching iron and driving tacks through from the outside.

The top ends of the cant ribs should be altered so they will not interfere with the ultimate fit of the outside gunwale, which must be able to flow naturally into the inwale near the end of the deck. This can usually be accomplished satisfactorily by tapering the very ends of the cant ribs from their full thickness at one edge to a reduced dimension at the other. This tapering is necessary only as far down the cant rib as the bottom edge of the gunwale, and it should be made on the inside surface of the ribs. It is done by scoring the bottom edge with a knife or backsaw just below the gunwale, then using a sharp chisel to complete the taper. The illustration shows the proper tapering for the White canoe, but the builder may have to make adjustments to fit his own particular model. The ribs are then fastened to the gunwale with nails, as were the regular ribs.

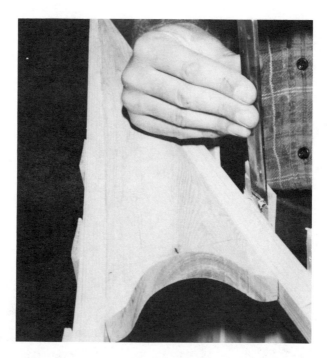

Tapering the tops of the cant ribs to provide a fairer entry for the gunwales. (P.H. DesLauriers)

Positioning the Thwarts

The thwarts are now ready to be secured temporarily in place. They are fastened to the gunwales with either ¼-inch bronze carriage bolts or 2″ x ³⁄₁₆″ brass machine screws used in conjunction with brass finishing washers. The thwarts are positioned directly on the ribs and squared with the hull accordingly. At this stage there is no reason to tighten down the bolts; it is necessary only to give the canoe shape and support while the hull is completed. Drilling the holes in the gunwale so that the bit angles very slightly "inboard" as it bores through is good assurance that the holes will not end up too close to the planking at the bottom. On the other hand, too much angle prevents the heads of the bolts from sitting squarely on the upper surface of the rail. The ends of the ribs that protrude unevenly along the gunwales can be trimmed down to within ⅛ inch of the rail with a sabersaw or a fine-toothed handsaw. When completing the cut, the builder must exercise care not to split the edge of the rib away. It is also important not to hold the saw at such an angle that the outside edge of the ribs actually will be cut below the level of the gunwale surface.

Completing the Planking

The planking job may now be completed. Usually only the sheer strake must be put on at this stage. Since it is impossible for a single plank to accommodate the sweep

Installing the cant ribs. When completed, they should look just like the bent ribs.

Cutting the rib ends close to the rail with a backsaw. (P.H. DesLauriers)

of the sheer without being cut to shape, working from the midsection of the canoe toward the ends is the best method of achieving the right pattern for this rather difficult area. At the ends of the canoe the sheer plank is cut away around the last 8 or 10 inches of the gunwale to allow the outer gunwale to lie up against it. This should be done neatly as depicted in the illustration. If the builder has chosen the mortise-and-tenon-style joint for the stem-to-deck union, the cut sheer plank should fit snugly along the underside of the inwale at the very end.

Now is a good time to cut the top edge of the planking the length of the canoe to match the lip that was previously milled on the outer gunwale. The depth of that lip, as described earlier, was ¼ inch; therefore, the planking should be cut the same dimension below the upper surface of the inwale. First mark the planking as illustrated, either with a compass that has an extension to ride flat along the inwale, or with a special jig that holds a pencil at the proper attitude to the planking while a flat surface is moved along the gunwale in the same manner. Then run the planking knife carefully along the drawn line, cutting the planking smoothly at the proper height with several passes.

Clinching the Tacks

By now you probably will have noticed that not all the tacks are turned into the ribs as well as they might be. The metal bands on the form served their purpose admirably enough, but as ingenious as the system is, it is not perfect. To hold

Fitting the sheer strake sections to complete the planking job.

A simple marking jig makes it easier to cut a neat line along the sheer plank.

The cut is made with a linoleum knife. The lip on the outwale should fit along this edge.

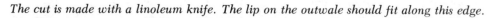

properly, the head of the tack must be driven firmly into the outside of the planking, and the tip must be not merely bent over, but actually curled into the surface of the ribs; so that there is no possible chance that the fastenings will loosen as the flexible hull works.

To be sure that all tacks are turned, use the clinching iron and go over the entire surface of the hull, sharply striking each tack while backing it up by the iron in the other hand. It is positively grueling work, but it is an essential job and fortunately not especially long-lasting.

Although the old-timers would laugh at such an unmanly approach, I find the job much less trying if the canoe is tilted on the horses to about a 35-degree angle by means of a line secured to one quarter thwart, wound around a spike in an overhead rafter, and run down to the other quarter thwart. This keeps the hull properly angled and balances it quite well even when I am working toward the very ends. The builder holds the appropriate surface of the iron against a section of the rib, bends over to spot the heads of the tacks on the outside of the hull, and strikes the proper ones with the tack hammer. Usually he is able to detect a soft, but full-toned, ring when the tack is properly struck. The builder moves the clinching iron along the rib from the garboard toward the sheer, turning it in his hand to match the changing surfaces, clinching all the tacks as he proceeds. When he reaches the sheer, he runs his fingertips along the rib to detect any imperfectly clinched tacks. Any renegades are treated once again with the hammer and iron.

The work is slow and awkward in the beginning, but with practice the job moves along with surprising efficiency, the hammer striking accurately, the iron positioned subconsciously, and the tacks singing their notes as they yield and bite into the wood. The superiority of the round-headed tacks becomes obvious at this stage. They burrow into the wood nicely with less visible damage to the wood, clinching properly with less effort. The hammer blossoms, which invariably occur during this operation no matter which type of tack is employed, need not be disturbing. They will disappear almost completely when hot water is slopped onto them to swell the wood back to its original form, provided the structure of the grain has not been seriously cracked—the sign of too vicious or too wild a blow. When one side of the canoe is completely clinched, the hull is tilted the opposite way, and the other side is treated in the same manner.

Installing Half-Ribs

On an 18- or 20-foot canoe, especially one destined for extended wilderness travel, a set of half-ribs will be a tremendous aid in extending the life of the craft. These light members are fastened along the bottom of the canoe between the regular ribs from stem to stem, increasing the lateral and linear strength of the bottom and creating a natural platform for keeping harmful dunnage up off the planking. The half-ribs can be bent onto the form itself and fastened as the planks are added if the form has metal strips for this purpose, or they can be put in at this stage of construction. Although it is faster and easier to bend them onto the hull after the two garboard planks have been secured, I have found it difficult to center the half-ribs properly and keep them straight using this method. Also, it makes the planking job more difficult, and the ends of the half-ribs are more likely to distort the planking.

The canoe is tilted at an angle to ease the arduous task of clinching all the tacks.

Using the clinching iron.

Much better results have been achieved by placing them individually into the completed hull.

The half-rib stock is planed to the same thickness as the regular ribs, then ripped to a width of 1¾₆ inches, and the edges are shaped in the same manner as the regular ribs. The lengths of the half-ribs vary as they progress from amidships toward the stems. The half-ribs should extend from bilge to bilge across the bottom of the canoe, not following the turn completely, but rather ending about halfway through it. Thus the ends of the half-ribs form a fair line along the center of the bilge on either side the whole length of the canoe, as illustrated.

Once cut to the proper lengths, the ends of the half-ribs must be thinned to allow them to conform to the shape of the bilge without distorting the planking. This can be done with a block plane or on the sanding drum. Both ends of the rib should be reduced on the bottom surface to half the original thickness over six inches of length. Thus any half-ribs less than 12 inches long will taper immediately from the center toward both ends. Finally the set of ribs is carefully sanded and labeled according to length, and the centers are marked on the upper surface.

Installing the half-ribs at this stage can be a one- or two-person operation. In the latter case the canoe is actually stood on its side on two horses so that the usual vertical axis of the stems is horizontal. It is secured to the overhead in the same manner as for clinching. The marked half-ribs are either placed in the steam box or set on end in a vessel of slowly boiling water. The whole set is frequently turned end for end to soak both ends thoroughly; in fact, each time a rib is removed from the vessel, the remaining ones are flipped over.

The builder facing the interior of the canoe controls the action. His helper is stationed along the outside of the hull to drive the tacks as directed. Taking the longest half-rib from the vat, the builder aligns the center of it with the seam between the two garboard planks. Taking care to place the half-rib evenly and squarely between the two full ribs, he drills two ¹⁄₁₆-inch holes through half-rib and planking, one on either side of the seam, then holds the clinching iron up to the holes. His helper, using the holes as guides, sets two tacks into place and drives them, clinching them securely against the iron held by the builder on the other side. Next the builders fasten the ends of the half-rib in the same manner, carefully placing the tacks no closer than 1¼ inches from the tip ends. The builder then drills a hole on either side of each planking seam the entire length of the rib; he holds the iron at each seam as his helper drives the tacks.

Each half-rib is secured in this manner, which, from my description, sounds less than efficient. In practice, however, once the two builders get into the rhythm of the job and straighten out their signals, the job flows along smoothly enough, and with practice, two people can install all the half-ribs in an 18-foot canoe in less than an hour and a half, getting them all straight, even, and with no split edges—something that can seldom be said for the alternate method of bending the half-ribs onto the form before planking.

The hull is now virtually finished except for sanding and installing the seats, which will come later. Hot water should be sloshed along each rib and half-rib on the outside of the hull to swell out the numerous hammer blossoms resulting from the clinching and half-ribbing operations. The surface is allowed to dry completely before sanding.

Placing the half-ribs in the hull to ensure that they form a fair pattern.

Installing the half-ribs singlehandedly. The boiled ribs are held in place with the clinching iron and the tacks are driven to fasten them in place. (P.H. DesLauriers)

The half-ribs in place. They add strength to the hull's bottom and also make a tighter platform for dunnage.

Dabbing hot water onto the planking to swell out the hammer blossoms.

Sanding the ribs with a short-based orbital sander.

Sanding the Ribs

The interior of the canoe offers only limited opportunities for finish sanding, which is why it is so important to presand all the pieces. Nevertheless, although nothing more can be done to the planking, the surfaces of the ribs and half-ribs can be greatly improved by a light sanding. The cant ribs and those immediately adjacent will have to be sanded by hand with 120-grit sandpaper applied with the grain, because no power sander will fit into the narrow confines of the ends of the canoe. The stem itself can also benefit from a light touch-up at this point. The remainder of the rib surfaces can be done efficiently with a small hand-held orbital sander with a 5-inch-square foam pad base. The foam pad allows the sandpaper to conform to the irregular surfaces inside the canoe. Run the machine along each of the ribs and half-ribs in turn, replacing the 120-grit sandpaper as often as necessary to keep it reasonably fresh. The contoured edges of the ribs themselves must be done very carefully by hand, using small pieces of 120-grit paper applied to the edges in such a way that the planking is not scratched across the grain. If this particular type of sander is not available, it is far better to take the extra time to do the sanding by hand rather than mess up the interior with an inappropriate or clumsy unit. It is far too easy to sand flat spots into the contoured interior even with light-grit sandpaper; do not take even a calculated risk. The pure white, satin interior of the properly sanded hull is sufficient reward for any pains taken during this step.

The ends of the canoe should be touched up by hand, since this area is difficult to do with any power sander.

Thinning the edges of the planking at the stem with a disk sander.

Sanding the Hull

It is equally important to sand the outside of the hull smoothly without taking off excessive material or flattening any curves. The most efficient unit for sanding the outside of the hull, at least initially, is a power disk sander with a foam pad base and 80-grit sandpaper. However, it is necessary to keep the machine moving to avoid grinding flat spots into such areas as the bilge. The builder should be aware of the fact that the foam disk actually bends during use and only a portion of the surface is being applied to the hull at a given time. Move the sander horizontally along the seams of the planking to eliminate the small ridges that are likely to develop, especially along the turn of the bilge. When you can no longer detect any protruding material by running your hand over the surface, change the direction of the application and move the disk across the hull laterally, further fairing the surface. Pay special attention to the ends; first smooth the face of each stem and the ends of the planking thoroughly by running the disk along the curved surface. Then, along the stem, thin the ends of the planking to about half their original thickness by holding the grinder at a slight angle to the surface of the planking. This reduces the width of the face by about one plank thickness. If the canoe were to be covered with fiberglass cloth, the corners of this stem would have to be relieved considerably to prevent air from being trapped under the cloth as it is folded over the sharp angle. With the canvas covering, however, it is necessary only to relieve the sharpest corners. A reasonably sharp corner is beneficial when it is time to pull the canvas tightly around the end for overlapping and tacking.

Final smoothing of the hull is accomplished with a long-based orbital sander and 60-grit sandpaper. The entire hull is faired with this finish machine, which is kept moving at all times and applied in numerous directions, depending on its location on the hull. The finished product should be a hull surface with smooth, fair contours, yet a slightly textured finish—especially if fiberglass is going to be applied as a covering.

A Desperate and Miserable Time

"A 16-foot canoe with 500 pounds of baggage and two men will draw about 6 inches. You must have that much water. Many Maine streams are less deep than that in the summer, perhaps they are 4 inches deep. A 20-foot canoe with the same weight will pass easily upstream where the short canoe cannot go at all. Many times I have come on young people having a desperate and miserable time in the summer months because of their short canoes. In my 20-footer I was passing with very little trouble and much pleasure.

"The 20-foot guide's canoe evolved over centuries of use by the Northeastern Indian. I do not think any other craft can equal them for versatility. I fear the short canoe is made for an unknowing and gullible public."

Mick Fahey
in an interview with Lynn Franklin

11

Canvasing and Filling

Canvasing the canoe is a straightforward procedure shrouded by an inordinate amount of mystique designed to make the amateur builder reluctant to try the job himself. The preparation for the task is actually more involved than the canvasing itself, and if the preliminary steps are followed, little difficulty should accompany the actual project. The materials and special tools necessary have been covered in Chapters 4 and 5. Briefly, the builder will need a length of the appropriate weight of canvas about a yard longer than the actual length of the canoe, a handful of the same tacks used to plank the hull, and a somewhat smaller number of the smallest copper or brass tacks available to do up the ends; $\frac{1}{4}$-inch or $\frac{3}{8}$-inch tacks are ideal for this purpose. Also important are the simple wooden stretching clamps described earlier, the two clothespin-like devices, the winch or come-along for pulling the canvas longitudinally, and artist's or upholsterer's fabric-stretching grips.

Canvasing the Canoe

The two wooden stretching clamps are suspended the proper distance apart with the lower ends 2½ or 3 feet above the floor. One of these is attached by a medium-weight length of chain to a wall of the shop, preferably to a strong horizontal crosspiece that will distribute the stress over several of the upright studs, or to another inanimate object such as a tree or the bumper of a parked pickup truck. The other clamp is fastened by a chain or cable to the winch, which is solidly anchored to another immovable object.

Even though you should have already vacuumed all surfaces and applied a wood preservative, it is a good idea to vacuum the hull once again if the shop is as dusty as most canoe shops I have visited.

Fold the canvas double along its entire length, forming an envelope into which the canoe can be slid once it is suspended in the clamps. Center one end of the
170

The folded canvas is stretched tightly before tension is released and the canoe is inserted.

folded canvas vertically in the wooden jaws; then center the other end, allowing an inch or two of extra cloth to protrude beyond the outside edges of each clamp. Tighten the grip by a combination of through-bolts and C-clamps until you are confident that the ends of the canvas cannot possibly be pulled free when the envelope is drawn tight by the winch. Use the winch to stretch the folded canvas until the surfaces of the envelope are perfectly taut and smooth and produce a solid thump when snapped with a finger. The uppermost edges of the fold must be even and uniformly taut. If one appears straight and rigid, while the other has a drooping sag in it, that is an indication that the ends were not clamped evenly, so the tension will have to be relieved and one of the clamps opened in order to remedy the situation.

When the canvas is satisfactorily clamped and tightened, the winch cable is marked at the drum with a bit of wire or string as a reference point indicating the proper tension. A bit of common sense must be applied during this exercise; the canvas must be pulled uniformly taut, but not so tight as to damage or actually rip apart the weave of the cloth, which can occur with continual, unrelenting tension with the winch. The proper degree of tension is achieved as soon as the wrinkles and sags disappear from the surfaces, and the tightening should then cease. It is also important to take the precaution of checking the inside of the envelope to make sure that nothing has fallen into the pocket. Anything inside could be trapped between the canvas and the canoe, causing a great deal of alarm and anguish later. Even a tiny sliver of wood or a shaving would stand out beneath the taut skin of the canoe like an embossed tribute to the carelessness of the builder.

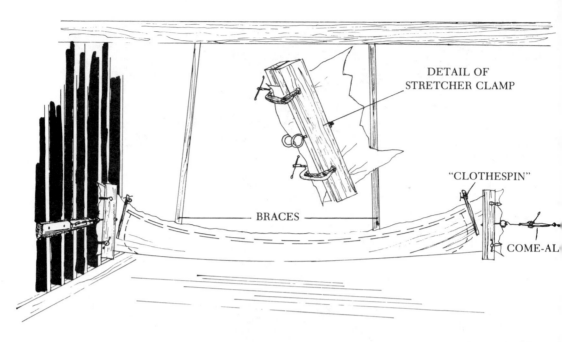

DETAIL OF
STRETCHER CLAMP

"CLOTHESPIN"

BRACES

COME-AL

Setting up for canvasing.

Next place the canoe inside the slack fold and push the ends as deeply into it as possible. Take up about half the slack with the winch. The more tension that is applied, the higher the hull rises inside its cocoon. Obviously, continued tightening would serve only to pop the canoe right out of its husk onto the floor.

With a blanket or similar cushion protecting the interior of the canoe, place a 6-foot board along the bottom of the canoe in each quarter. The boards should be positioned as close to the ends as possible but without allowing the edges to wedge between the sides of the canoe where they could actually bite into the wood. The boards serve as a protective platform for the builder, who actually climbs into the swinging canoe, driving the hull deeper into the canvas fold.

Two staunch uprights about a foot longer than the actual distance between the bottom of the canoe and the overhead are now employed to brace the canoe down into the canvas from the overhead. This will result in lateral tension on the fabric, as the canoe is forced down into the fold to complement the linear tension being applied by the winch. By walking back and forth from one end to the other on the protective platform, the builder can make sure each of the braces is wedged securely in place. His assistant can then slowly take up more cable with the winch until he approaches the mark indicating proper tension.

Still swaying in the unsteady hammock, the builder continues to drive the canoe down by decreasing the angles at which the braces are set, until they are nearly vertical. A few more turns on the winch handle, to exceed the original mark slightly, should make the canvas tight enough for tacking. Most of the wrinkles should be eliminated by now, with the exception of a small fold along the bottom at each stem. If a fanlike pattern of wrinkles runs diagonally from the stem to the wood

The canoe rests in its canvas cocoon.

The canoe in its white hammock, braced and ready for tacking the canvas in place. (C.R. Tuttle)

stretching clamp, the vertical tension provided by the braces is too strong in relation to the horizontal tension. Easing off a bit with the uprights and taking a turn or two on the winch should bring the two into better balance and eliminate most of the wrinkles. The two jumbo clothespins made from the hardwood sticks can now be jammed over the edges of the canvas at the ends of the decks to bring the canvas in this area alongside the inwale. The canvas is then trimmed the whole length of the canoe to within three inches of the sheer line.

To tack the canvas along the sheer, the builder works from the midship rib toward the ends. At each rib, he grips the edge of the canvas as close to the sheer as possible with the stretching pliers or grips; using a wood scrap to protect the gunwale, he pulls up slightly, then rocks the head of the pliers back onto the gunwale about 45 degrees. The ¾-inch tack is positioned in the center of the rib, ⅛ inch below the trimmed edge of the sheer plank, which is visible as a slight ridge beneath the taut canvas. The tack is driven into the inwale through canvas, planking, and rib. If the proper tension has been applied, a small, tight fold or lip will materialize just above the head of the tack when the grip is loosened. Too little tension will result in the absence of this lip or even a sag below the head of the tack. Too much tension is evidenced by a very tight, hard pucker directly above the tack and a general scalloped look between the tacking points as the job progresses. This condition is difficult to spot at this stage, but it becomes very noticeable along the outside gunwale after the gloss finish paint is applied.

The builder proceeds with the pulling and tacking along the sheer toward the end until he reaches the deck; then, beginning again amidships, he works toward the opposite end. The other side is treated in the same manner. Before relieving the tension, the builder inspects the job carefully to make sure that no wrinkles remain and that nothing has been trapped between the hull and the new skin. Only then can the canoe be removed from the canvasing rig. The extra canvas above the tacks is not trimmed until the filler has been applied and allowed to cure.

Doing the ends up properly is a bit more challenging than the first part of the operation. This overlap will represent the only seam in the skin below the waterline, so great care must be exercised to make the joint neat and completely waterproof.

Set the canoe upside down on the horses to facilitate this operation. Determine a point along the flat run of the stem in a direct line between the last tacks driven into the sheer on each side. With a sharp utility knife, make a slit from this point along the imaginary centerline of the stem and out to the end of the canvas. This cut produces a separate flap of cloth on each side of the stem; these must overlap each other on the stem face to make the required waterproof seam. Drive a tack at the head of the slit to keep it from running farther, then pull the two flaps taut linearly, overlapping them at the very head of the slit and driving five or six of the small tacks through both layers ⅜ inch apart. The first inch or two of the slit is thus securely overlapped and firmly fastened.

From here, work with the bottom layer, folding the top flap back out of the way. Gripping the edge of the flap every three inches or so, pull the cloth normal off (or 90 degrees to the curve of the stem at each point) tightly around the face of the stem and tack it. Space the tacks about ¾ inch apart and arrange them in a neat row just to the far side of an imaginary centerline running down the face of the stem. This makes it possible to tack the second flap of cloth right along the centerline and still overlap the first.

The builder then tacks the first flap along the whole length of the stem right up to the protruding gunwales. Then he is able to finish tacking the canvas along the sheer on that side. He employs fabric pliers again to pull the canvas tight at each of the remaining ribs (normally the two cant ribs are all that are left) and drives one final tack near the end of the gunwale. This last step should result in a tight-fitting, smooth skin at the end of the canoe.

Using stretching grips to pull the canvas tight for tacking. Note the protective wooden button on the gunwale. (P.H. DesLauriers)

Fastening the canvas while holding it with the stretching grips.

The little fold directly above the tack head indicates the correct amount of tension. (P.H. DesLauriers)

The builder then trims the excess canvas on the stem neatly and carefully along the very edge of the tack heads with the utility knife. He then treats the face with an application of the weave filler before the second flap is lapped over it and tacked, using his fingers to work the mixture into the weave. The row of tacks for this second flap is placed just to the far side of the row beneath it to form a tight, waterproof seam approximately in the center of the stem face. When the second flap is completely tacked, the builder holds out the excess cloth perpendicular to the stem face and cuts it off as close to the tacks as possible, taking great care not to slice the bottom layer by accident. If the blade is sharp, the seams will be neat and straight, requiring only filling to become an unobtrusive, completely waterproof part of the total skin. The remaining end of the canoe is tacked in the same manner. When completed, the pure white shape of the canoe resembles the back of a great marine mammal, sleek and smooth, without a ripple to distort its gracefully efficient form. It is easy for the builder to imagine how smoothly the craft will move through its intended element.

(Continued on page 184)

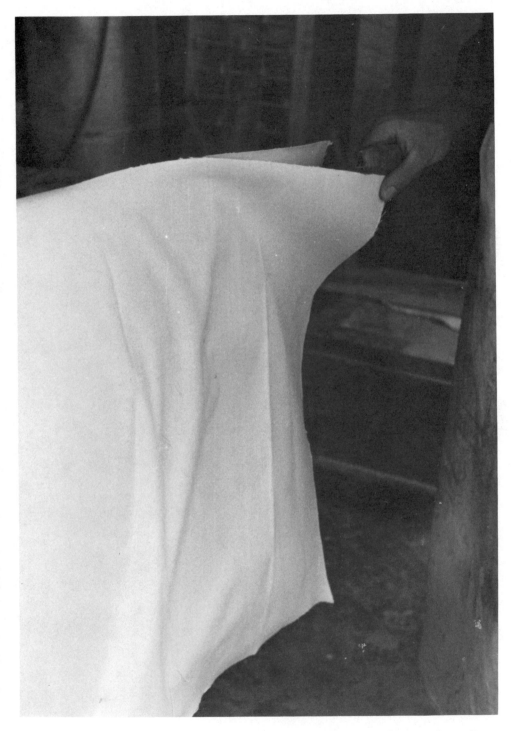

The canvas has been slit at the end and the two resulting flaps are ready for tacking. (P.H. DesLauriers)

Tacking one edge of the canvas at the end.

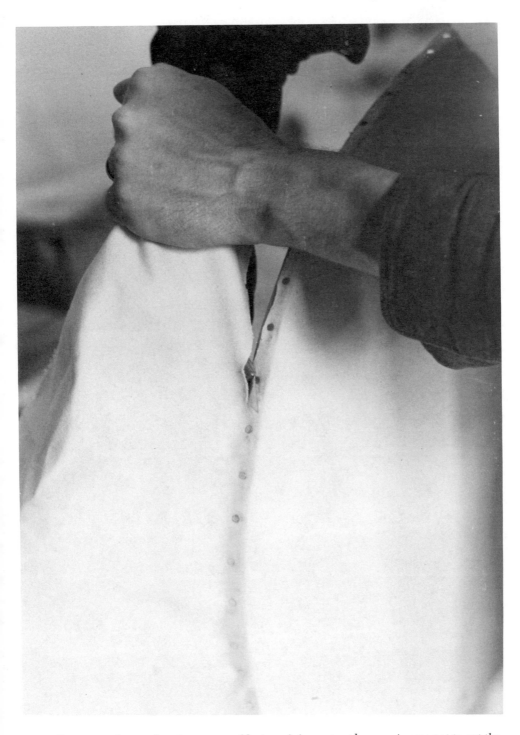

Carefully cutting the overlapping canvas. Neatness is important here, as is care not to cut the layer underneath. (P.H. DesLauriers)

One side is all tacked, trimmed, and treated with filler. The overlapping flap is ready to be tacked.

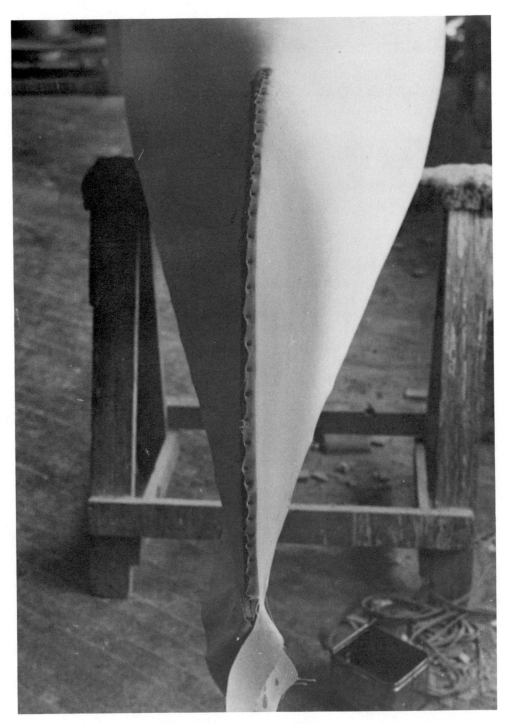

The overlapping flap is tacked.

Filling the Canvas

Even the best canvas will have an odd burr or two and be covered with an inconspicuous lintlike fuzz, both of which inhibit the weave filler from doing its job efficiently. A light scorching of the fabric with a standard propane torch effectively minimizes the problem. The builder holds the torch nozzle parallel to the surface of the hull, an inch above the surface, and allows the flames to glance off the canvas, igniting the nap and carrying the tiny cinders away in a shower of sparks. The torch is kept moving at all times along the surface laterally, one section at a time, until the whole canoe has been done—brown singe marks will cover the hull uniformly. Any small burrs should receive an extra dose of the flame treatment to reduce them, but care must be taken not to heat them to the point where they will themselves ignite when the flame is removed and burn a disastrous hole completely through the fabric. It is also advisable to watch the loose threads along the rough edge of the canvas at the sheer, because these ignite easily and can burn a little furrow right up the side of the canoe.

Filling the weave is a simple but grueling job that taxes the builder's physical stamina as well as his skill. Still, if he applies a few principles to the task and resigns himself to its physical rigors, he should end up with a very satisfactory job. The filler is designed to waterproof the covering; provide a tough, smooth surface for painting; resist abrasion; and add overall strength to the wood-canvas system. Unlike the traditional white-lead-based fillers no longer available, the modern commercial preparations have an oil base and generally are less likely to crack after exposure to the elements. The filler is only as effective as the filling job, however, so having procured a suitable quantity of the mixture (a few sources are listed in the Appendix), the builder should concentrate on doing a thorough job and letting the filler take care of itself. Before beginning the task, a few loose-fitting mitts should be made from the leftover scraps of canvas.

The canvas will need at least two and probably three applications of the filler, but these are applied consecutively, with no drying time required between coats. It is best to do one three-foot section of the canoe at a time, with a generous overlap as the work progresses. The filler must be thoroughly mixed as specified in the directions before you begin. The first coat is applied with a stiff-bristled 5-inch brush. The one I prefer has the bristles cut off to a length of about 1½ inches, but this is not necessary for a one-time application. Apply the mixture liberally to the section being treated and work it vigorously into the weave with both circular and back-and-forth strokes. It will soak into the canvas quickly, and the surface will soon appear dry but still very rough.

Immediately brush on a heavy second application and use the canvas mitt to work the filler into the cloth. This requires a good deal of physical exertion, but this second coat must be completely rubbed into the weave. The surface should now appear smooth upon casual examination, with none of the fabric pattern readily visible. Upon close scrutiny, however, there will probably be a few rough, scalelike patches where the filler is thin and the fabric pattern somewhat discernible.

(Continued on page 190)

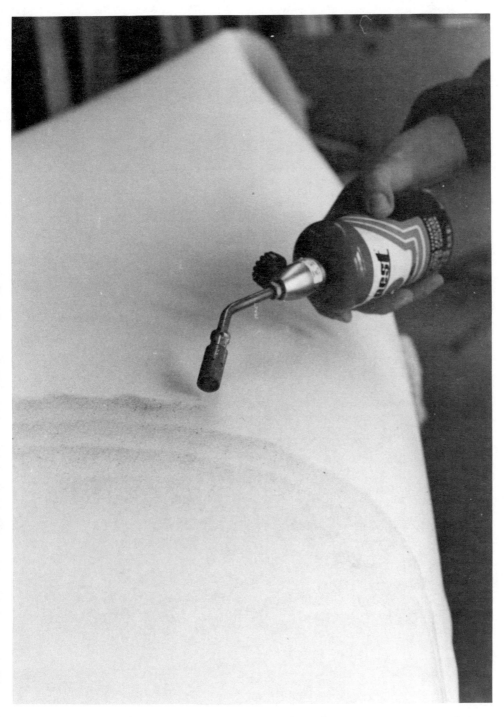

Scorching the canvas to remove the nap and tiny burrs. (P.H. DesLauriers)

The scorching completed.

The author applying the initial coat of filler with a circular motion of the brush. (Lynn Franklin)

Rubbing in the second coat of filler with a canvas mitt. (Lynn Franklin)

Smoothing the third and final coat of filler with a bare hand. (Lynn Franklin)

The filling job is completed—a gratifying moment in the canoe-building process. (C.R. Tuttle)

Although these spots may seem inconsequential at this stage of the operation, they will be sorely obvious when the final paint is applied, so they must be dealt with beforehand. Thus, a third coat cut with 10 percent paint thinner is applied lightly with the brush and rubbed in once again with the mitt until the surface appears smooth and almost dry. The filler can then be groomed with bare hands to a true satin smoothness, eliminating any spots that were not completely filled.

Then proceed to the next section, overlapping the first generously and repeating the same steps to achieve the smooth finish desired. The mitt should be discarded when it becomes completely clogged with the compound.

By the time the builder has covered the entire surface of the hull in this manner, he will be ready to call it a day's work. The care and patience that have gone into this step, however, will be graphically reflected when the canoe is finally sanded and painted. The seams at the ends of the canoe must be treated with repeated applications, with the overlap filled completely until there is no sign of an open seam.

The filler requires a long curing period of between two and three weeks at 70 degrees F. Colder drying temperatures can lengthen even this period substantially. The filler is designed to maintain its flexibility within the weave, but the surface becomes hard and slatelike when cured. It is fully cured when a thumbnail scraped across the end of the stem scratches the surface without penetrating it, much as it would the surface of a chalkboard.

Metal Canoes

"When the canoes began to change, then the whole thing changed. When the first aluminum canoes and plastic canoes come out, well, none of the real guides was going in any of that, didn't go with it."

Myron Smart

"That old White of mine, canvas, had the same load as he did, and I went down the same river, didn't hurt it a damned bit. Oh, I knocked some shellac off the bottom. It give enough and come right back in place. . . . Christ, they tried to pound the crookedness out of that tin canoe, brand new too, and they couldn't do a thing. I used my canoe like that 20 years, and it was still just right at the end of it."

Myron Smart
in interviews with Lynn Franklin

12

Seat, Gunwale, and Keel Installation

Although it is somehow more sophisticated or north-woodsy to paddle a canoe from the kneeling position—as anyone who has attended summer camp in the past 75 years will tell you—many people, myself included, find it much more comfortable in all but the roughest water to paddle while seated. As previously discussed, numerous fibers are available to weave a durable and comfortable seat, and some prewoven materials serve the purpose equally well. These include natural cane, both in strands for weaving and in prewoven fillers, nylon or neoprene cord, and rawhide strips such as those used on snowshoes. The fiber chosen influences the size of the stock necessary to build the seat frame. The dimensions given in the chapter on milling stock ($\frac{7}{8}$ inch molded and $1\frac{3}{8}$ inches sided) apply specifically to a seat frame grooved to accept the prewoven natural cane fillers. A hand-woven seat requiring a large number of holes in the frame should be $\frac{1}{4}$ inch wider and perhaps $\frac{1}{8}$ inch thicker.

Seat Installation

The lengths of the bow and stern seat frames normally differ because of their relative placement in the canoe, to achieve a good balance as well as provide adequate leg room. The stern seat is traditionally placed well back near the stern deck and is suspended much closer to the gunwales than is the bow seat; both factors give the sternman better visibility by holding him higher above the water. It can also be argued that this likewise raises the paddler's center of gravity, thus adversely affecting the stability of the craft. Still, to my way of thinking, it is quite as important to be able to see where one is going as it is to keep one's weight near the bottom of the canoe. In fact, in moderate rips, the sternman gets a much better picture of the route ahead by standing up and using a long-shanked paddle or his setting pole.

194

Cutting tenons with a dado head on a table saw.

At any rate, the builder will have to weigh for himself the merits and disadvantages of raising the stern seat, and make his own decision on exactly where to place the seats. On the White canoe in this book, the stern seat is located at the fourth and sixth true ribs from the end, with the wider span measuring 18 inches, while the bow seat is just ahead of the bow quarter thwart at ribs 11 and 13, with the longer piece measuring almost 29 inches. The width and length of the seat itself are the same for both, since there is little difference in backside width, whether one is paddling bow or stern. The inside measurements of the seats themselves are 10¾ inches in width (across the beam) and 7¼ inches in length. The pieces are joined by either mortise-and-tenon joints or dowels, the first method being the stronger of the two.

The crosspieces that span the canoe are cut to the longer of the two relative lengths, in this case 19 inches for the stern seat and 30 inches for the bow. The shorter connecting pieces are cut at 8⅝ inches to allow for a ¾-inch tenon at each end. The tenon itself is ½ inch thick and 1 inch wide. The tenon is carefully marked on both ends of the short stock as in the figure, then the material is removed carefully on the table saw or bandsaw, or with a fine-toothed backsaw and a sharp chisel.

The mortises are located on the longer struts and carefully centered and marked to the correct dimension. A ½-inch brad-point drill bit is first used to remove most of the material from the mortise. The depth to which the bit penetrates the wood

Removing most of the material for the mortise with a wood bit on a drill press.

must be carefully controlled by the stop on the drill press, or by marking the bit with a strip of tape if an electric hand drill is used. Two holes directly alongside each other will remove nearly all the material, then a sharp chisel is used to square the corners and otherwise dress the mortise until it is neat and clean, and the tenon fits tightly into it.

A good waterproof glue with either a resorcinol or an epoxy base is then applied to both pieces at each joint, and the frame is carefully fitted together and clamped until dry.

The groove is routed or the holes drilled into the completed frame before final shaping and sanding. A simple wooden frame, properly dimensioned to take into account the radius of the router base, makes a good pattern for guiding the router along the pieces of the frame. The groove should be situated evenly around the frame. The width and depth of the groove depend on the size of the spline to be used to hold the cane fast. The edges of the seat frames can then be relieved with either a router or a block plane and rasp, and the frames sanded smooth.

The 12-inch-wide prewoven cane is the proper width to accommodate the seat frames just described. It is cut to the proper length, allowing ¾ inch to extend beyond the groove on all sides. Any cane fibers that run parallel and overlap the wood should be removed with an awl to prevent the cane from bunching on the surface of the wood. Only fibers running perpendicular to the frame should be allowed to span the wood. The trimmed cane filler is submerged in a pan of warm water to allow it to soften and stretch. The natural fiber splines are cut to length with mitered corners and also placed into the water to soften.

The tools necessary to insert the cane filler are a tack hammer, a small section of hardwood with a spine or tongue cut into it (to force the cane down into the groove), waterproof glue, and a sharp chisel.

When the cane has been allowed to soak for at least 20 minutes, the mat is centered on the frame. With the opposite edge held in place as tightly as possible, the builder forces the long edge of the filler into the appropriate groove, using his tongued block and simple hand pressure, working carefully from the center toward each end. He then forces the fitted spline into the groove to hold the cane temporarily in place. Moving to the opposite side, the builder drives the cane into the groove with his special wooden block and hammer, again working from the middle. He then cuts the loose ends of the cane with the chisel along the far inside corner of the groove and removes the severed ends. He draws a bead of waterproof glue along the bottom of the channel, sets the spline into place, and drives it in tightly with the hammer, using a piece of wood to protect the fiber from the actual blows. Returning to the first side, the builder removes the spline and then the cane from the slot, then reinserts the filler, this time using the hammer and wooden block. He cuts the long ends with the chisel, applies the glue, and drives the spline into place. The two shorter edges of the cane can then be inserted into their respective grooves in the same manner. When the job is done properly, there will be no sags or bulges even in the wet cane, and when it dries, it should be absolutely drum-tight.

The varnished seats are best installed in the canoe after it too has been finished; otherwise they will interfere with the varnishing process. After determining their

Clamping the seat frames after applying glue. (The stove is not burning.)

Routing the groove for the woven cane filler.

A wooden tongue on a hardwood block for driving cane into the groove.

The cane filler cut to size; outside strands have been removed.

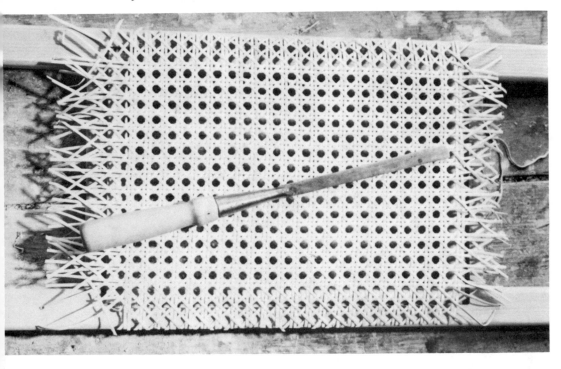

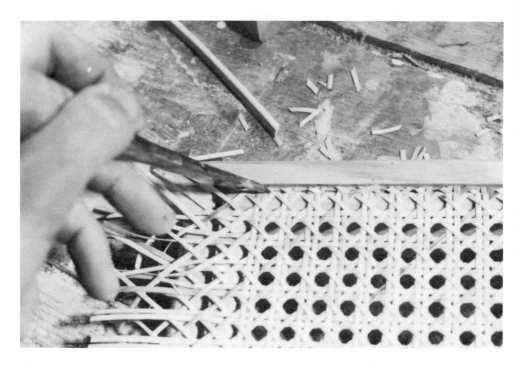

Cutting the long fibers after driving them into place in the groove.

The two long sides of the cane trimmed and the splines in place.

Placement of the stern seat.

proper location, the builder centers the seats on the gunwales. The proper length, which corresponds to the outside edge of the inside gunwale, is marked, and the angled cuts are made. The fitted seats are then suspended the proper distance below the gunwales by means of wooden spacers cut from ¾-inch dowels with holes drilled through the center, and the carriage bolts or machine screws. On our canoe, the spacers are 1⅛ inches and ⅞ inch for the bow seat, and ¾ inch for the back strut of the stern seat. The front member of the stern frame is bolted flush with the gunwale. The rise of the sheer determines the relative difference between the two spacers for any one seat, and it has to be adjusted to each particular model so the seats will be level.

Gunwale Installation

The outside gunwale can be installed as soon as the filler is dry. The canvas must first be cut very carefully and neatly along the top edge of the sheer plank. Any bit of canvas fiber sticking above this line will cause the canvas to bulge slightly when the rabbeted outer gunwale is clamped into position. Beginning at the center of the canoe, the builder fits the lip of the gunwale snugly down onto the top edge of the sheer plank and clamps it into place. Then he works carefully toward each end, fitting the lip carefully along the top of the planking and making certain the top surfaces of both gunwales are even at any given point. It is sometimes necessary to place a length of soft wood across both gunwales and tighten it down with a clamp on the inwale until the top surface of the outwale is forced into the same plane. The lip of the gunwale must be tapered to nothing at the very end so it will sit flush against the surface of the inside gunwale where the planking has been previously cut away. This tapering can be done best with a block plane.

When a half section of the gunwale has been clamped into place, the builder fastens it with either 1½-inch or 1¾-inch No. 8 bronze or brass wood screws at every second rib. Before fastening, however, it is advisable to check the canvas along the bottom edge to be certain it has not been forced down into a noticeable bulge at any spot. The screws need be countersunk only enough to set the flat heads flush with the gunwale surface, except near the ends of the canoe, where they should be deep enough to allow the builder to taper and fair the outwales with a block plane into a fair and pleasant entry (see illustration).

The very ends of the ribs, which now protrude a small fraction of an inch above the gunwales, can be taken down with the belt sander until flush. The builder should use a light-grit belt and take great care not to tilt the sander forward or backward on the rib ends and inadvertently grind unsightly scallops into the surfaces of the gunwales. Once the top surface has been sanded smooth, a router or a block plane can be used to achieve a slight radius on both rails. The gunwales and rib tops are then hand-sanded until perfectly smooth and coated with a clear wood preservative.

Keel Installation

If a keel is desired, it should be made and installed at this point. This seemingly insignificant strip of ash is surprisingly effective in stabilizing the craft as well as increasing its ability to track on open bodies of water. The keel also protects the canvas, especially when the canoe is drawn up on a beach. On the other hand, the keel is a decided menace in heavy rapids, because it limits the paddler's ability to draw the whole canoe or even the bow sideways, and these are frequently critical maneuvers. In light to moderate rapids, the adverse effects of the keel are not so apparent.

The one-inch-deep-by-⅞-inch-wide keel extends the length of the hull from where the stem begins its upward curve to the same point at the other end. It should be hardwood, preferably ash because of its lightness. Normally the sides of the keel are slightly beveled so that its face is only ⅝ inch wide. The contact surface is hollowed to accommodate a good application of bedding compound when the keel is installed. The depth of the keel diminishes at the ends from the full inch to only 3/16 inch at the tip over a distance of about 15 inches so that it flows gently into the natural shape of the stem. The width of the keel also diminishes at the ends from full width to the approximate width of the metal stem band that will be used on the stem itself.

The sides of the keel can be neatly beveled on the table saw; the tapering at the ends will have to be done by hand with a block plane. The hollow on the contact surface can be achieved with either a router or a shaper or by running the stock across the slightly raised blade of the table saw at a slight angle, allowing the blade to remove material nearly the whole width of the keel in one pass. When approached from such an angle, the circular blade cuts a perfectly uniform hollow.

The gunwale clamped in place for fastening.

A small device for marking the precise placement of screws on the gunwales.

The stock must he held down firmly and set against a temporary wooden guide clamped at the proper angle across the surface of the table. The depth of the cut should not exceed ¼ inch.

When the ends have been tapered and the keel sanded, it is ready to install. First a chalkline must be struck the length of the canoe—not down the exact centerline, but precisely half the keel width to one side of the centerline. The edge of the keel is then set along this chalkline, ensuring that the keel is straight and true.

The 1¼-inch No. 10 bronze or brass screws fasten the keel in place from the inside of the canoe. Generally a fastening is placed on every second rib, and brass finishing washers are used to prevent the screws from penetrating too deeply into the surface of the rib. The hollow surface of the keel should be filled with a good marine bedding compound, and each screw should be dipped into this substance before fastening.

The actual operation is done with the canoe resting upside down on the sawhorses. One person is needed to hold the keel firmly in place on the hull. The builder himself is beneath the canoe, carefully drilling the holes up through rib, planking, and canvas and into the keel; he secures the screws with their finishing washers in place. The builder uses the garboard seam as a guide to place the fastenings properly. The keel is fastened starting from the middle and working toward the ends up to the stem itself. The very ends of the keel are fastened from the outside, using a smaller-number screw that is long enough to penetrate the internal

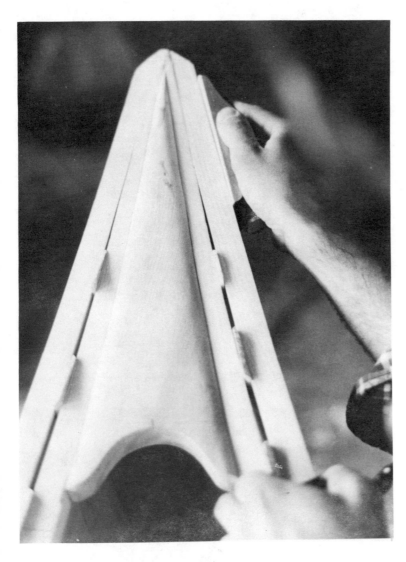

Tapering the gunwale with a block plane to achieve a more finished look.

stem of the canoe without going through it. Any bedding compound that has been squeezed out onto the hull during the process should be carefully removed with a putty knife and, finally, a small amount of paint thinner on a rag.

The end seams of the canvas must be protected by some sort of metal strip or stem band. Since the overlapped seam makes the surface of the stem face uneven, it is necessary to use a band that has a concave inside surface. The hollow holds the bedding compound and spans the actual seam, while the edges sit squarely on the flat of the stem face. A flat-backed stem band teeters on the seam and cannot trap any of the compound. At one time many fine brass stem bands were available, but with

Belt sanding the tops of the ribs and upper surface of the gunwale.

Cutting a hollow in the contact surface of the keel by passing it at an angle over the slightly raised blade of the table saw. (P.H. DesLauriers)

The bulk of the keel is fastened from inside the canoe, using finish washers to prevent the fastenings from burrowing into the ribs too far.

The ends of the keel can be tapered in thickness and width with a block plane.

The keel in place on the filled canoe, awaiting finishing.

the decline in popularity of canvas-covered boats, they have become truly difficult to find. In the complete absence of a suitable brass protector, I have resorted to ⅜-inch-wide concave-backed aluminum bands.

The bands must be properly drilled and countersunk to accommodate ⅝-inch

No. 4 or No. 5 round-headed wood screws about every five inches. The length of the stem band should correspond directly to the length of the stem, and the builder should take care that the last screw is not placed beyond the end of the wooden stem inside the canoe. If the canoe has a wooden keel, the stem band should be run right up the tapered face of the keel for several inches. In either case, the end of the metal band must be filed to a gentle bevel to prevent it from catching on something and ripping off.

More On Poling

"But there comes a situation when the water is too strong or too shallow to paddle back against it, you can't hold yourself on the paddle and you are out of control. Whenever the depth is such that the paddle top hits bottom, stop paddling. A paddle is a piece of sculpture to be cared for. That's when you have to use a pole. A pole is strange to many modern canoeists, but a fundamental tool for a woods canoeman. He wouldn't go anywhere without it. It's about 12 feet long. With a pole you snub the canoe, push the light stern—your bow is heavy with baggage and draws more than your stern for descending a shallow, rocky, swift river—and set it so the current automatically swings the bow into line with the stern. You set your pole, shove the stern to the right, hold it there, and the bow will swing directly in line. Same for the left, you snub pushing your stern left and hold it. Clear of the obstruction, you release your pole and let the canoe drop forward.

"This is the safest method of descending swift, rocky water. You must never fight the river. Your strength is infinitesimal to the power of the water. You must let the current do the work for you. There is no other way. It is very easy to position your light stern and hold it with a pole and let the current align your bow. Then you drop down a few lengths and repeat the procedure to avoid the next rocks. You are using your experience and knowledge, not your strength to maneuver. And you can manage safely in very rough water."

Mick Fahey
in an interview with Lynn Franklin

" . . . An experienced man propelling his canoe with a pole is an unexpected and moving sight as he rhythmically works his way upriver, reading the current, using eddies and rocks, shifting his weight to guide the canoe. It all looks so effortless and natural, touched with the distinct flourishes of pole handling, a blend of years of application and personal temperament. It is one of those moments in which a whole way of life can be revealed."

Herb Hartman
The Canoeist's Catalog

13

Finishing the Canoe

The purpose of all the extra care and sanding invested in the canoe thus far has been to achieve a handsome finish on the final product. There is no reason why a functional item cannot be beautiful as well, and the project will be that much more gratifying if the builder remembers this as he applies the protective finishes to both the interior and the exterior of the canoe.

Finishes

The interiors of wood-canvas canoes were once coated with a tough spar varnish, which provided a beautiful, glossy finish when new. Unfortunately, it required almost yearly stripping and reapplication; otherwise the heavy varnish would build up in thick layers that would check badly and eventually flake and peel, requiring a heavy-duty stripping agent and a great deal of messy work to remedy.

Some builders still prefer spar varnish, claiming that it provides the toughest shield against severe weathering conditions. Most, however, have switched to one of the marine polyurethane finishes, many of which contain a partially effective ultraviolet shielding ingredient to help them better withstand the ravages of direct sunlight. Polyurethane flows on thinly, making it easier for a beginner to achieve a reasonably good finish. The resulting buildup is also considerably less; with normal use, the original finish is serviceable for several years—with the possible exceptions of the gunwales, which receive the most exposure. Even after this period, it is often possible to renew the luster and protective qualities of the finish by thoroughly cleaning the surfaces of the wood, sanding lightly with a medium-fine-grit sandpaper, then simply adding a new coat.

Before using either type of finish it is prudent first to treat the carefully sanded interior with an application of the appropriate grain sealer. The sealer is extreme-
212

ly fluid, penetrating well into the wood and filling any pores, which otherwise would soak up much of the first application of the varnish itself. The sealer can be applied with either brush or rag, and although the builder need not be as fussy as with the actual varnish, this is no place for careless work.

If mahogany has been used anywhere on the canoe, it is a good idea to apply a stain-filler/paste combination. This product seals the relatively open grain of the mahogany and darkens and enriches the color uniformly.

Finishing the Interior

Before varnishing, the builder removes the thwarts and places them aside along with the seats for separate treatment, thus allowing better access to the interior of the hull.

Applying the varnish itself requires all the care and patience the builder can summon. The atmosphere should be as dust-free as possible, although this is seldom a reality in a small, multipurpose shop. Even if the canoe has been sealed the previous evening, it is necessary to vacuum out the interior and carefully go over it with a tack rag. The instructions on the product label should be read and heeded, particularly those regarding temperature and humidity tolerances. Most recommend against any application in a cold or damp atmosphere. Likewise, even though it may seem appealing to move the canoe out into the bright sunlight for better ventilation and a chance to work on a suntan as well, it is difficult to obtain good results under such conditions. The sunlight begins to cure the varnish almost as it leaves the can, making it thick and sticky on the brush and almost impossible to put down smoothly. It is also more difficult to control dust and tiny flying insects outside than it is in the shop; and finally, no one does his best detail work while being baked by the sun with sweat pouring off his brow amid numerous welcome yet concentration-breaking distractions.

A natural-bristle brush, preferably one with an oval-shaped head, is generally considered the best tool for laying down either type of varnish. One that is about 2½ inches wide works best for me. A smaller brush for finishing the little rectangular openings between gunwales and ribs is also necessary. Apply the varnish in clean, smooth strokes, avoiding mashing the bristles into tight spots as much as possible, as this causes inevitable runs down the sides of ribs and planking. The peaks up under the decks must not be neglected, nor the undersides of both gunwales (unless the builder chooses to paint the undersides of the outer gunwales instead, which is acceptable practice).

Under ideal conditions, the first coat will have cured well enough by the following morning to allow the builder to prepare the interior for the second coat. This preparation usually involves a light but very thorough sanding of all surfaces, followed by vacuuming and tacking the surface. The results of the second coat are much more dramatic than those of the first. The interior starts to gleam with a smooth luster that reflects the light readily and highlights the natural tones and grain patterns of the cedar. For most satisfactory results, however, a third coat should be added, again after light sanding with a fine-grit paper or fine steel wool, and thorough cleaning. It is this third application that provides a tough shield capable of resisting scratching and bruising during normal use.

The thwarts have been removed to facilitate finishing the interior.

After the finish cures, the varnished thwarts and seats may be installed, and as long as the builder continues routine care, he can look forward to a finish that shows off his careful handiwork to best advantage for years to come.

Again there are always exceptions, and some builders still advocate finishing a canoe with natural oils only. These builders maintain that repeated applications of boiled linseed oil or a combination of boiled linseed oil, turpentine, and pine tar prevents the wood from becoming brittle and also eliminates the problems of a varnish buildup. There is no doubt that repeated applications of the oil will do much to maintain the cedar's resiliency, but the oil itself will eventually turn the wood nearly black, guaranteeing the owner a different sort of refinishing problem in the future.

Finishing the Exterior

The exterior of the canoe must also be protected. The dried filler itself is not designed to withstand prolonged direct exposure to the sunlight and should also be protected from scratches as much as possible.

Builders have long relied on marine enamel paint to provide such protection. Although these paints do demonstrate outstanding weathering properties, they do not dry to an especially hard finish, a deficiency that I consider very serious, given the use (and abuse) to which most canoes are subjected. To achieve this desired hardness, many old-timers in northern Maine painted their canoes with a com-

The sealer seals the open grain and brings out the tones in the wood. (P.H. DesLauriers)

bination of porch and deck enamel and automobile paint—a mixture that would no doubt give a paint chemist much to ponder. In addition to this combination, many guides would shellac the canoes below the waterline, a coating that allowed the hull to slide more easily over obstacles, and one that could be renewed quite easily each year after sanding and scraping the old coat.

We have had our most satisfactory results with straight acrylic enamel auto paint, a finish that has good weathering properties and is very tough.

The two-part epoxy paints are lauded by some manufacturers as adhering especially well to the filler as well as providing a nearly indestructible finish. Epoxy paint does, however, have the reputation of being somewhat difficult to apply. I cannot assess the accuracy of these statements, having never experimented with the stuff myself.

Before any type of paint can be applied to the cured filler, the builder must make proper preparations. The surface of the canvas is now very hard, almost like slate, and smooth at least to the casual observer. A light peach fuzz may be distinguishable over portions of the hull—the result of nap that wasn't sufficiently scorched. A light sanding with 80-grit sandpaper is necessary before applying the recommended primer. For an extra-smooth finish, the hull may be coated with a

The completed canoe embodies all the grace of the original E.M. White design.

yacht undercoater or surfacing paint, which is very thick in consistency and fills the minute hollows and valleys that would otherwise go undetected until the finish coat blatantly emphasized them. These surfacing paints dry quickly and sand easily with regular aluminum oxide sandpaper. The paint can be applied carefully by brush, or it may be sprayed on with a spray gun.

When the primer or undercoater is dry, the builder sands the entire hull with 120-grit paper. As the paint is removed, the hull takes on a mottled appearance; the high contours become gray as the filler is exposed, and the low spots retain the white undercoater. The surface of the sanded hull also becomes progressively smoother. After a second application of the surfacing paint, much less sanding will be required to produce a true smoothness with very little gray showing through. If the finish paint is to be applied with a spray gun, the hull should be sanded further with 240-grit paper.

The builder thins the finish paint as directed and applies it carefully with a good brush. If he is going to use a spray gun, the builder must mask the gunwales and hang a protective skirt of newspapers from the rails of the inverted canoe to prevent the spray mist from contacting and settling on the finished interior. Two light coats with the brush will produce better results than one thick one; with the spray gun method, however, sufficient coverage can be achieved with one application. The art of spray painting is well developed and practiced by many automotive specialists, but it is something that I have never enjoyed or ever felt very confident doing. For those who have the talent, it can pay off handsomely in a mirrorlike protective coating, guaranteed to earn anyone's admiration. It is important to allow the paint to dry to its maximum hardness—a process that may take up to several days—before using the canoe.

The canoe is now complete: the reflection of all the pains, tribulations, and triumphs of the builder. No one will fault him for taking a few moments to admire the craft that he so painstakingly created, as it rests, proudly gleaming, atop the sawhorses. Yet the canoe doesn't truly come into its own until it is properly launched into the element for which it was intended, where it floats gracefully and trimly. Aboard it, through the medium of wood and canvas, the owner experiences a unique relationship with the dynamic, pulsating hydrosphere and everything that is a part of it.

"Actually, it is only in the woods and along the rivers or sailing on the bay or ocean that I feel secure and self-confident. Back in the city, I have to place my security and welfare in the hands of others, and the result is that I am too dependent upon too many people to feel comfortable about it. Even when exploring a new river in my canoe or threading my way through an unknown forest, I know where I am and, if not where I am going, at least how to return."

Dale Rex Coman
Pleasant River

14

Rebuilding an Old Canoe

The rigors of canoe construction may be more than some readers wish to tackle at this point. This doesn't mean they must do without a good wooden canoe, even if they haven't the capital to invest in a new one. Thousands of old wood-canvas canoes can be found scattered throughout the country; many are serviceable as they are, but most require at least some attention. Restoring such a canoe can be a rewarding project for anyone who is interested in learning about the craft and who can solve a variety of intriguing problems as they turn up. Broken ribs, cracked planking, worn-through canvas, and a dull finish can all be dealt with by almost anyone with some perseverance. Rotted stems and decks and broken inner gunwales present another level of challenge, but when approached logically and carefully, they can be remedied satisfactorily. Restoring the entire canoe to authentic mint condition represents another level of undertaking, which is best reserved for experienced craftsmen who have a great deal of time and expertise to invest in the project.

Patching the Canvas

Patching minor tears in otherwise adequate canvas is not at all difficult. A clear, fast-drying plastic cement such as Ambroid, used with a scrap of light cloth, can make an unobtrusive, effective patch on such a blemish. Such repairs can be made right on the banks of the river during a canoe trip, and the voyageur can be back on the water in less than half an hour.

To make such a repair, first rough up an area about the size of the patch with a fine-grit sandpaper. Then apply a layer of glue to the surface, filling the rip itself as much as possible. Next apply the patch and fill the weave with the glue,

220

New gunwales, decks, canvas, and a few ribs will do a lot to restore an unusable craft to full service.

smoothing it with a bit of wood or a fingertip. When the glue is dry, the edges of the patch can be faired smooth with sandpaper and the surface painted, making a neat and very functional patch.

Removing Old Canvas

More likely, especially if the canoe is an old one, the canvas itself is weak and the filler cracked, and both should be replaced. Besides, if much repair work must be done to the woodwork itself, it is important to remove the canvas to effect such repairs.

Since the canvas is not actually bonded to the hull, removing it is quite easy. The outer gunwales, stem bands, and keel (if there is one) must first be removed by taking out the screws that secure them in place. The tacks that fasten the canvas along the sheer and the stems can be removed singly, or the canvas may actually be ripped along the rows of fastenings and a standard tack puller used to remove fragments of cloth and the tacks. Before recanvasing the hull, it is a good policy to go over the craft and reclinch any loose fastenings or replace those that have broken tips. If fastenings are either loose or broken, the heads of the tacks will rub their way through the new canvas as the canoe works. Likewise, any stripping of the interior finish that requires a chemical agent should be completed before the new canvas filler is applied—for obvious reasons.

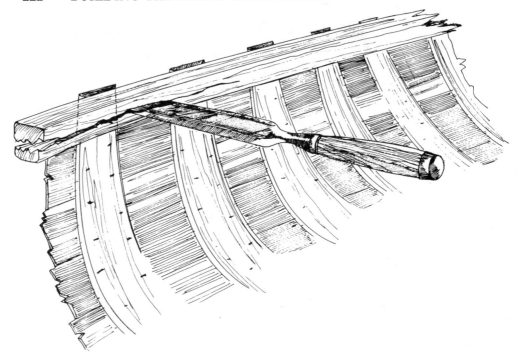

Splitting away a gunwale.

Exposing Dry Rot

It is not uncommon to find some dry rot in the very ends of an old canoe; this often involves the decks, the gunwales, and the tops of the stems. Dry rot cannot simply be ignored, and it must be dealt with while the canvas sheathing is off. Sections of the two or three topside planks must be removed to get at the area properly. The best method is to cut the planks back on alternating ribs, then remove the tacks and break them free at the stems; the nails securing the planking to the stems hold so tightly that it is nearly impossible to unfasten the planks without destroying them. The punky decks can be removed by unfastening the screws that secure them to the gunwales.

Should only the very tips of the gunwales need replacing, it is possible to execute a solid splice along the edge of the new deck itself, eliminating the need to replace the entire gunwale lengths. If the inwales need replacing, they should be removed at this time.

Removing the nails that hold the ribs to the gunwales without destroying the upper inch or so of the ribs is virtually impossible; therefore, it is better to cut the inwale into several short sections and then either split the inwales away from the fastenings with a chisel and mallet or cut the nails with a hacksaw after prying the end of the rib away from the rail with an old chisel. In the former case, the exposed nails can then be snipped flush with snub-nosed clippers.

Repairing Stems

The extent of dry rot in the stems is usually limited to the top 3 to 6 inches. Rather than try to replace the whole stem—a major ordeal—you can make a neat, strong, splice at this point. When carefully done, it results in a renewed stem that is truly adequate for full service.

The first step in executing this splice is to cut off the top of the stem at an angle, leaving a long, diagonal surface onto which the new section of ash or oak can be securely bonded. A V-notched piece, which actually backs up the existing remnants, as shown in the illustration, allows the piece to be screw-fastened from both directions. In combination with a waterproof glue, this method creates a very strong splice. Naturally, the new top section is beveled to match the existing stem.

Replacing Gunwales

A new inwale, preferably of spruce, is milled out to match the old rail. If the canoe displays tumblehome (that is, if the sides of the craft pull in toward the centerline at the sheer) the gunwales are sure to have a bevel cut along the outboard surface. This bevel should be reproduced, as should any tapering in width that might occur at the ends of the originals.

Clamp the new inwales into place along the tops of the ribs and secure them with ¾-inch or ⅞-inch bronze ring nails or galvanized ring nails, two at each rib. Then screw the new decks into place after applying marine bedding compound to the edge surfaces. The joint with the stem at the ends may be made as described earlier in this text, or the builder can duplicate the canoe's original system. In many models, the stem simply is run up by the deck, which has had the point squared off to match the width of the back surface of the stem.

Repairing Planking

Rotted planking is rare because of cedar's excellent resistance to rot. Any sections that are cracked across the grain, however, should be replaced while the opportunity exists. Minor splits that run with the grain may be ignored except for adding a few tacks along both sides of the split and drilling ³⁄₃₂-inch stop holes at either end. The bad sections should be cut away, locating the butts at the centers of the appropriate ribs. The planking should be cut with a linoleum or utility knife held at a 45-degree angle to the surface of the hull. This allows the builder to make bevel-lapped butt joints by matching the bevels on the replacement sections. Remove the tacks with great care, rolling the head of the puller in the direction of least resistance to minimize damage to the ribs. When replacing sections of planking in areas of tight turns, such as the turn of the bilge, hot water applied to the outside surface will prevent the plank from splitting. Install the garboard planks along the centerline, as described in the chapter on planking, with much hot water and firm, steady, hand pressure.

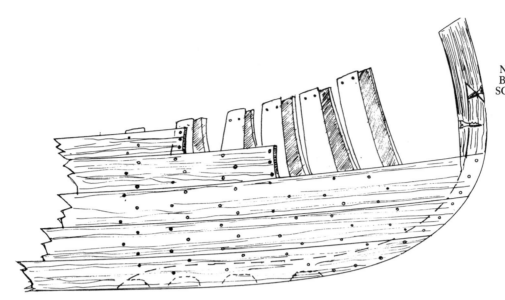

1"
NO. 6
BRASS
SCREW

Detail of a strong stem splice.

Removing a section of planking.

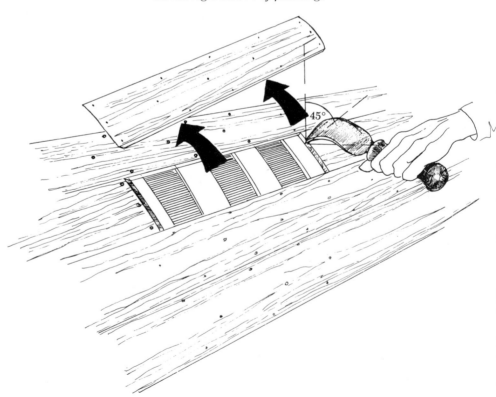

45°

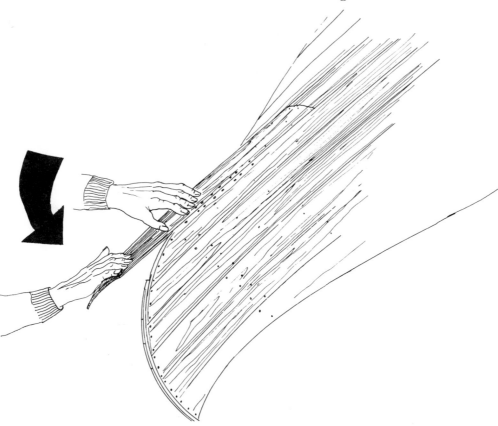

Bending a wetted garboard after nailing it along stem.

Replacing Ribs

Cracked and broken ribs present no major difficulties, but they should be removed as carefully as possible. Straighten out the tacks from the inside with the tack puller before trying to pull them through. If the gunwale hasn't been removed, the fastenings that secure the ribs to the gunwales must be cut or the rib split away. Tilting the flat bottom section of the rib amidships and pulling steadily is the best method of freeing the ends between gunwale and planking. If there are a number of badly damaged frames in a row, only every second one should be removed for the first steaming; otherwise it is extremely difficult to install the new ones without distorting the shape of the hull.

Mill the replacements to reproduce the original members exactly, then steam-soften the ribs in some sort of chamber. For this limited application, use a section of metal stovepipe, capped on the ends, with wire forming a grate inside for separating the ribs to ensure maximum exposure. The steam can be generated in a kettle or similar vessel placed over a wood or propane flame and channeled into the stovepipe through rubber tubing. As mentioned earlier, submerging the cedar

Removing a rib by tilting it amidships and applying steady pressure.

ribs in water just prior to steaming them tends to increase their capacity to absorb the steam.

When the ribs are supple, remove them from the chamber, bend them snugly around the corresponding section at the opposite end of the canoe, and clamp them in place for about a minute. This preshapes the frame roughly and makes fitting it into its slot much easier. Install it by tilting it to get the ends between gunwale and planking; then slide it into place before it stiffens and hardens permanently. To get the rib to fit the contours of the hull precisely, apply downward pressure to the top of the rib with the palm of the hand while holding the center portion in place. Extreme care must be taken not to distort the planking by exerting too much pressure. Once the rib is fitted and clamped into place, fasten it with the brass canoe tacks.

Interior Refinishing

If the overall condition of the canoe warrants such an endeavor, the builder may choose to refinish the interior woodwork, a painstaking and messy job at best.

Using downward pressure to force a rib into its proper shape.

Because of the problems imposed by the complex nature of the interior, the only feasible method of accomplishing this is to employ a chemical stripper. Such an agent, if meticulously applied and removed with putty knives, scrapers, and steel wool, can effectively eliminate the built-up varnish and produce a reasonable finish. The newly exposed wood should then be sealed and protected with three coats of a good marine polyurethane or spar varnish, sanded lightly between coats. The darker spar varnish better complements the darkened golden tones of the old wood.

Recanvasing and Completing

Canvasing the restored hull is no different from canvasing a new one, as already described. When the filler has cured, the keel, outer gunwales, and stem band material can be replaced. Some canoes with keels are equipped with outside stems of wood. Since these frequently are troublesome spots, it may be necessary to replace them. Mill out the stock before soaking and cut a hollow into the bearing surface, as described in the chapter on keels. Steam or boil the stock and bend it around the curve of the stem, as in the figure, and allow it to cure. Then join the flat run of the stem to the keel with a scarf joint.

The dried canvas filler should be prepared and painted exactly as described in Chapter 13. Once rebuilt, the canoe is capable of many more years of full service and will display the special qualities expected of such a craft. If he gives it respect and reasonable care, the owner will have a trusted friend for a lifetime and will still be able to pass it along intact to the next generation of voyageurs.

Upriver

"I loved it and learned the river, learned not to be terrified by the roar of turbulent water, to keep my head when slipping back down the cataracts, just keep pushing for a hold and when I got it to call John to get ready, that I was right behind him, and to shove like a John Deere tractor, and then go on. I love poling and I love the big White canoe. The cedar ribs do not oilcan at all, but keep their fluid, beautiful, round shape and give just a little under your feet, so you can feel what you're working with. You can lift and drop the bow by stepping forward and back; step back to enter the cascade, step forward after halfway up it, step back for the next cascade, and on and on with the rhythm of serious and dedicated canoe polers. We did the poler's dance—UPRIVER FOREVER!"

Lynn Franklin
The Canoeist's Catalog

15

Making Paddles and Poles

Paddles

It is still hard to beat a rock maple beavertail or Maine guide-style paddle for general pleasure and serviceability. When carved to the right proportions, such a blade is supple, durable, and a joy to behold. It is also surprisingly light and will last indefinitely if given proper care. It is not, however, designed for fending off rocks in the rapids or pushing along the bottom in the shallows; the first situation should be avoided as much as possible, and the setting pole is the tool for shallow-water travel.

Oak, ash, spruce, or poplar can also serve well for paddle material. Straight-grained spruce makes a wonderfully light paddle with good flexibility, but it is not as strong as the hardwoods. However, one can compensate for this shortcoming by making the shaft a little larger than normal for a hardwood paddle. Poplar is easy to carve and very light and has a certain amount of spring, but it is not especially strong or particularly resistant to rot.

Blade width is another important consideration. Up to a point, a wider blade gives the paddler better performance and more thrust than a narrow one, but for cruising, anything over 8 inches is probably too wide. Seven inches is a popular width, and even 6 or 6½ inches is good for a young paddler.

Paddle length is generally determined by the paddler's height and his position in the canoe, although this may not be the case with every canoeist. The old standby rule is chin height for the bow paddler, eye height for the stern. Try this for starters, but don't be satisfied until you find the length that feels most efficient and comfortable.

The tools of paddle making are few and simple for anything but production work. All you actually need are an axe and a block plane. Having the luxury of an

230

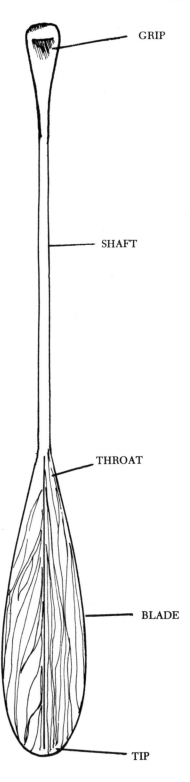

GRIP

SHAFT

THROAT

BLADE

TIP

Parts of a paddle.

equipped shop, however, I rely on a bandsaw for cutting out the silhouette, then a combination of drawknife, smoothing plane, and spokeshave for carving. The drum sander makes final shaping and sanding relatively easy. Those who are skilled with a crooked knife generally prefer it to anything else for the carving job.

Having arrived at a suitable design, the builder traces his pattern onto the stock—which has been selected for its absence of knots as well as its straightness of grain—and planes it to 1⅛ inches in thickness. He carefully cuts out the shape of the paddle on the bandsaw, just outside the line. Then he places the paddle in a vise and fairs the shape exactly to the line with a spokeshave.

The blade must be thinned from nearly full thickness at the throat to about ⅜ inch just before the slightly bulbous tip itself. These represent the dimensions at the very center of the blade; the edges are further thinned to about 3/16 inch. A cross section of the throat of the paddle would be somewhat elliptical in shape. Near the tip, this ellipse flattens and lengthens out considerably to the full 8-inch width of the paddle.

To achieve this shaping, the builder clamps the paddle to a bench or sets it in the vise and uses a drawknife and hand plane to rough out its dimensions, first on one side and then the other. He first carves away the edges with a drawknife, creating a bevel, which the hand plane can utilize as it is applied ever closer to the center of the blade.

Because of the shape of the paddle, the grain on one side of the centerline will usually run opposite to the grain on the other, requiring the opposite angle of approach with the carving tools. Final shaping is done with the block plane and spokeshave.

The shaft itself is shaped with a spokeshave. The shaft is not perfectly round, but rather measures the full 1⅛ inches front to back and slightly less than an inch in width. This gives the shaft more strength and makes it more comfortable to the hand as well.

There are a number of grip styles, varying chiefly in length. Most are scooped out on both surfaces to accommodate the palm and fingertips, yet to provide a substantial grip at the very top, reducing muscle fatigue in the hand. The hollows are rough cut on the bandsaw and finished with chisel and spokeshave.

The whole paddle is then sanded smoothly from grip to tip. The drum sander is excellent for this job but certainly not essential. If the paddle is to be polyurethaned, give it at least three coats, allowing it to dry and sanding lightly between coats. The grip itself is not varnished, a precaution that lessens the risk that the paddle will raise blisters during use. The alternative is to treat the paddle with two coats of boiled linseed oil, allowing the first coat to soak in thoroughly before applying the second. The paddle can then be conditioned as often as necessary simply by adding more oil. The oiled paddle, for my money, is better looking and certainly more comfortable to use.

Setting Poles

Despite the great excitement over the relatively new aluminum setting poles, I see little to recommend them for anyone interested in wooden canoes. Wooden setting

The paddle grip, roughed out on the bandsaw, awaits further finishing.

A spokeshave works best for carving the blades of paddles made from hardwoods such as maple.

Sanding the paddle on the drum sander.

The finished paddle. It is finished with varnish on the blade and linseed oil on the shaft and grip.

poles, either naturally grown or turned on a lathe, have been used successfully for generations, and although they are not indestructible, they should serve the tradition-minded canoeist very well.

The naturally grown poles have much to recommend them. Usually of black spruce, they are extremely strong because of the natural circular pattern of the grain; they are light if they are not too green; and they are readily available along most waterways, at least in the northeastern part of the country. Some woodsmen suggest they be cut from trees that are dead, but still standing, because a green setting pole will check badly. The trick is to find one that is not too dried out or already afflicted with dry rot. The slender trunk, which should have a diameter at the larger end of about 2¼ inches, is cut to 11 or 12 feet in length and limbed. It is then peeled and the limb knobs are smoothed as much as possible to protect the poler's hands. Usually the only protection applied is natural hand oil as the pole is used, although such a pole would surely benefit from a coat or two of boiled linseed oil as it dries.

I find two disadvantages to the natural poles: (1) they tend to be tapered dramatically, and although it is good practice to pole with one end only, it is sometimes convenient to use the other end in a tight spot, and the narrow end is often too small to take such strain; (2) try as one may, it is nearly impossible to get the knots smooth enough for true comfort until the pole is so well worn that it is nearly time to replace it.

Clear ash poles turned on a lathe are normally 1¼ or 1⅖₁₆ inches in diameter along their entire length. These poles are strong, supple, smooth, and light, and either end may be used if required. Overall, they may be the best poles available, and with minimal care they should last a lifetime.

Unfortunately, few shops are equipped with lathes capable of handling 12-foot stock, but this does not mean the builder has to do without a first-class, smooth, ash or spruce setting pole, provided he can locate a long enough piece of stock that is free of knots. If ash is used, a 1⁵⁄₁₆-inch square strip should be ripped from the selected stock; if spruce is to be used, it is ripped 1⅝ inches square. The four corners are then cut away on the table saw, with the blade set at a 45-degree angle to achieve an octagonal cross section. A smoothing plane can be used to accomplish this same end. Once the spar is eight-sided, it is relatively easy to round it by applying a block plane or a spokeshave. Final smoothness is achieved by hand sanding first with 80-grit and finally 120-grit paper. Two applications of boiled linseed oil provide the best finish for such a pole.

The butt end of a tapered, naturally grown pole, and both ends of a straight one, should be protected by some sort of metal shoe. Forged pick-pole tips from river-driving days or tips of peaveys or cant dogs (used for rolling logs over) are old standby favorites for tipping a setting pole. Such a metal tip is less likely to slip on gravelly bottoms, and it also protects the wood. However, many enthusiasts find such fittings difficult to locate today, and they are unnecessarily noisy in rocky streams, with their monotonous clanking each time the pole is set.

A better alternative is an inch-long section of appropriate-size iron pipe, which is fitted over the end, with about ½ inch of wood protruding from it. The pole is shaved so that the metal ring fits snugly; then the end of the pole is split on the

Sawn poles ready for rounding.

An effective pole tip consisting of an iron ring and a hardwood wedge. The protruding wood will mushroom, further securing the ring.

Trying out the canoe on a quiet stream.

bandsaw to allow a wedge to be driven into it. The metal ring is then heated for a few minutes with a propane torch and driven onto the pole as far as possible. Too much heat will cause the ring to burn the wood, resulting in a looser rather than a tighter fit. Then the hardwood wedge is driven in and the excess wood cut off to within ½ inch of the metal. This wood may be "mushroomed" slightly with a mallet in the shop for further holding power, although one use in most streams is all that is required to mushroom the wood sufficiently. An advantage of the metal ring tip (with the protruding wood), beyond its availability and its ability to keep the wood from splitting, is its sound-dampening effect.

Outfitted with his hand-crafted paddle and pole, the canoeist removes himself still further from the consumer-oriented weekend sport; and the careful work and patience will pay off in many years of pleasurable service from a pair of fine-looking river companions.

Rowing a Canoe

"Boats that are good paddlers also make good rowing boats. As a matter of fact, an admirable pulling boat is a canoe. Rowing is definitely a vastly superior way of canoeing compared to paddling, as anyone who has fitted oars to his canoe can tell you. The marked increase in propulsion efficiency is particularly welcome when going to windward, and can be quite exciting when heading off the wind in a breeze. In the last condition, if you pull hard just as a wave is lifting her stern, you can scare yourself with speed."

Roger Taylor
The Canoeist's Catalog

16

Building a Sailing Rig

There are two different approaches to canoe sailing. One is geared toward serious competition, complete with specially designed canoes, massive sail areas, hiking boards, formulas, handicaps, regattas, great excitement, and finely tuned skills. The other approach is much more casual: a standard canoe hull is equipped with a medium-size lateen or lug rig, leeboards, a paddle for steering, and a make-do, enjoy-the-experience attitude. Not that the latter is totally without its rewards and excitement. Any canoe with the sheet cleated fast, slicing the waves on a windward tack with spray drenching the occupants, can provide a large measure of exhilaration for all aboard.

Anyone with a canoe and a desire to experience this enjoyable and sometimes useful art can put together a suitable outfit without going heavily into debt. Several manufacturers produce sailing rigs that are reasonably good, not terribly expensive, and adaptable to any canoe. The lateen rig from any of the popular little fun-sailers can also be fitted to a canoe and made to sail satisfactorily.

Starting from scratch is certainly the most intriguing approach, however, and for someone who has just built or rebuilt a wooden canoe, this is probably the way to go. A lateen rig is a good choice because it is surprisingly efficient, while still simple in concept and design. In addition, the short mast requires neither stays nor shrouds. The amount of sail area will depend on individual requirements. For a short canoe 16 feet or under, or for a reasonably portable outfit to help traverse some of those long, windy, wilderness lakes, 45 square feet is probably sufficient. On the other hand, someone who plans to sail his 18½-foot or 20-foot canoe seriously, and has a bit of experience behind him, can handle 80 or 90 square feet of sail. A typical cruising or pleasure rig for a 17- or 18-foot canoe should carry about 60 square feet of sail area, and this is the outfit discussed in this chapter.

For the sail material itself, the builder has a choice between Dacron and cotton. Dacron, although extremely durable, is neither as traditional nor as aesthetically

242

The lateen rig on an 18½-foot White canoe, which has been especially adapted for sailing, with deck, coaming, rudder, and a single leeboard.

pleasing as cotton. However, if extensive voyaging is part of his plan, the cruiser will definitely appreciate the carefree qualities of the synthetic.

I have never made my own sails, but I understand it is somewhat more involved than cutting out and fashioning throw rugs from burlap feed sacks. I have always been able to buy custom-made sails at what I considered reasonable rates from professional sailmakers, who demonstrated great skill and took much pride in their work. The resulting sails not only were very pleasing to the eye but fit the other parts of the rig and trimmed nicely without sags or bellies. I do know of people who have made their own sails, however, achieving varying degrees of success, and the necessary information is available in a number of texts.

Like anything else, the sail has various parts, each with its own term, and knowing these allows the canoeist to chat with his yachting counterpart over cocktails without sounding too much the fool. These are all listed on the diagram and should need no further explanation. The triangular shape is not perfectly equilateral; thus the angles are not a uniform 60 degrees. Instead, the angle at the tack is 63 degrees and the remaining two each 58½ degrees. The corners of the sail must be reinforced and fitted with large grommets for securing the sail to the spars. The tack is cut in a radius or arc with two grommets, one for attachment to the gaff and the other for attachment to the boom. In addition, the sail has a row

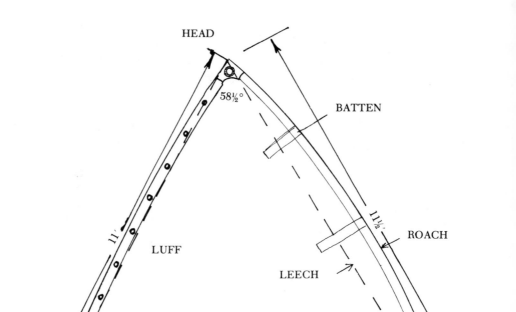

Parts of the sail.

of grommets 10 inches apart along both luff and foot, allowing it to be lashed securely to the spars in a spiral manner. Three pockets for holding ⅛-inch-thick ash battens are spaced uniformly along the leech of the sail. The battens are 2 inches wide. The center one is 15 inches in length, while the two outside ones are each 12 inches long. The leech of the sail is not cut as a straight line, but rather as a fair arc called a roach, which adds about 8 inches of cloth to the triangle at its widest point. A mild arc of about 3 inches maximum width is also cut along the luff and the foot.

The spars for this rig are few and simple and should be constructed of clear spruce, laminated if necessary to achieve the necessary thickness. The mast for such a rig is 8½ feet long, with the thickest section 2 feet from the step or a few inches above the point where it passes through a thwart specially made for support. From 2⅜ inches at this point, it tapers gracefully to a diameter of 1½ inches at the top. The lower portion of the mast tapers to a 2-inch diameter, ending in a 1-inch-long square tenon at the bottom. The tenon fits into a corresponding mor-

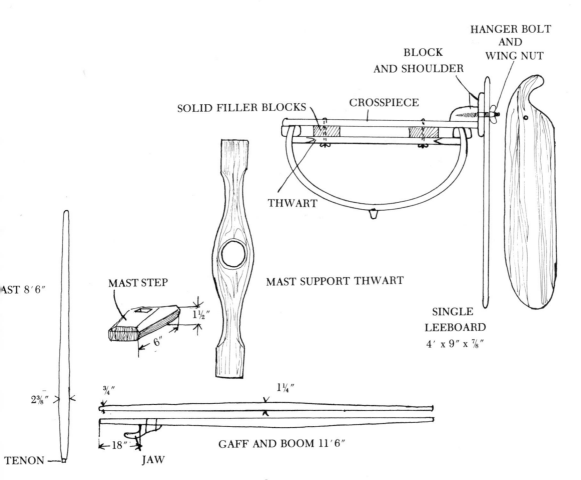

Parts of the rig.

tise in a hardwood mast step. The tapers can be cut from square stock on the table
saw; the rounding is done with a block plane and spokeshave. The gaff and boom
are 11½ feet long, tapering from 1¼ inches at the center to ¾ inch at each end. A
single jaw, cut from hardwood or bent into a piece of metal such as ½-inch half-
round brass, is through-bolted to the boom with ³⁄₁₆-inch brass machine screws. It
should grip the mast 18 inches from the boom tip, allowing spars and sail to protrude past the mast by this amount in classic lateen fashion.

The two spars must be joined in some manner that allows them to pivot open
when the sail is set, and to close when not in use and when being transported. A
thick leather strap, lashed or riveted to each spar, can serve this function. We normally use an L-shaped flat fitting that is cut on the bandsaw from ⅛-inch bronze
stock. The long section of the "L" is riveted with two rivets along the end of the
boom, while the perpendicular foot is riveted with one rivet to the gaff. We use
large-gauge bronze nails for rivets, clipping the ends and mushrooming them with
a ball peen hammer onto the surface of washers on the other side of the spar. The
single hole in the gaff itself is drilled large enough to allow the joint to pivot

A flat bronze fitting for joining the spars with a pair of bronze nails that are used as rivets.

smoothly. Holes are provided at the distal ends of the spars for tying off the spiral lashing, which is $\frac{3}{16}$-inch soft nylon or Dacron line.

Also secured to the gaff 6½ feet above the joint is a small eyebolt to which the halyard snap is secured for raising the sail and holding it close to the masthead. Locating the eyebolt a bit above the mathematical center of the gaff enables the sail to be tipped forward, allowing the skipper and passengers more headroom aft. The yoke or jaw grips the mast 2½ feet above the step, allowing the tack to clear the canoe even with the sail carried at this angle. Near the very top of the mast on one side, a small single block and pad are mounted for the halyard.

The mast is stepped approximately 3½ feet from the stern of the canoe. An especially wide thwart with a hole cut in it is bolted in at this point, or in some cases a specially designed stern seat with an extra-wide forward crosspiece and a hole can be located at this position. Small, thin hardwood wedges serve to make the mast fast at this critical point, preventing it from shifting around as the sail shifts. The mast step itself is a small rectangle of hardwood 1½ inches thick with the mortise cut into it for the foot of the mast. It should be long enough to span two ribs. If it is built into the canoe, the contact surface is bedded, and it is fastened from the outside of the hull with a pair of 1½-inch No. 10 bronze wood screws. In a canoe with canvas intact, it may have to be glued to the ribs with epoxy glue after the varnish has been removed from the spot. If the canoe has an outside keel, it can be fastened into this. The holes are drilled from inside and the screws are liberally coated with bedding compound before they are inserted.

For lateral resistance, a pair of leeboards can be fashioned from mahogany or ash, although a single long board will serve nearly as well. The overall length of the single board is 4 feet—about 3⅓ feet of which is below the pivot point. It is 9 inches wide and shaped from a ⅞-inch piece of wood. In cross section the leeboard should resemble an airfoil, tapering in thickness to about ⅜ inch at the trailing edge. The leading edge corners are also relieved heavily to minimize drag through the water. The single leeboard is surprisingly effective; even when it is on the windward side with the canoe well heeled over, enough of the board remains in the water to minimize leeway as well as to maintain proper trim.

If two leeboards are preferred, they should be 38 inches in overall length and 8 inches wide. They may be fashioned from ¾-inch stock. The leeboards must be attached to the canoe at the correct balance point in a manner that enables them to work without putting undue strain on any part of the canoe. A double thwart best fits these particular requirements.

The proper position for the boards can be determined only by actual experimentation. A crosspiece with a 2″ x 4″ x 6″ wooden block secured at each end can be temporarily clamped across the gunwales approximately 2½ feet aft of the mast. A vertical 1-inch-thick wooden plate is fastened to the end of each heavy block to provide a shoulder for the leeboard to pivot against. The leeboards are affixed by means of ½″ x 6″ hanger bolts that screw into the plates and blocks and are threaded on the exposed ends to accept large wing nuts and washers, which hold the leeboards in place yet allow them to swing up if they hit an obstacle or encounter shallow water.

Distributing the weight of all aboard to simulate normal sailing positions, the skipper sails the canoe into a good breeze. He then removes his paddle from the water and notes the response of the canoe. If the bow falls off the wind, the boards are too far aft and must be moved ahead. For safety reasons, the canoe should turn into the wind when stopped, but the leeboards should not be more than a few inches ahead of the actual balance point. Conveniently, with the 18½-foot White canoe, this point corresponds to the position of the forward quarter thwart. With the addition of a pair of filler blocks set between quarter thwart and crosspiece and two carriage bolts, the leeboards are securely mounted in the proper position. Should the balance point not be located so easily, it may be necessary to cut and reposition a thwart slightly for this purpose, making it a relatively easy job to secure the crosspiece whenever the sailing rig is required.

The running rigging (in addition to the 3/16-inch lashing cord) consists of a halyard of ¼- or 5/16-inch nylon or Dacron line 30 feet long and an identical sheet.

In addition to the small single block and pad at the top of the mast, another is located just above the thwart on the aft side of the mast for the sheet and one other about 2½ feet from the end of the boom. A ¼-inch eyebolt located on the forward deck serves for further running the halyard. A small cleat located under a thwart convenient to the skipper makes raising and lowering the sail easy and safe, and a jam cleat to accommodate the sheet once the sail is set allows the sailor the use of both hands to manage the steering paddle, yet he still has the ability to release the tension on the sheet quickly if required.

The halyard is clipped to the eyebolt on the gaff, then run through the block at the head of the mast, down to the eyebolt in the forward deck, and aft to the skip-

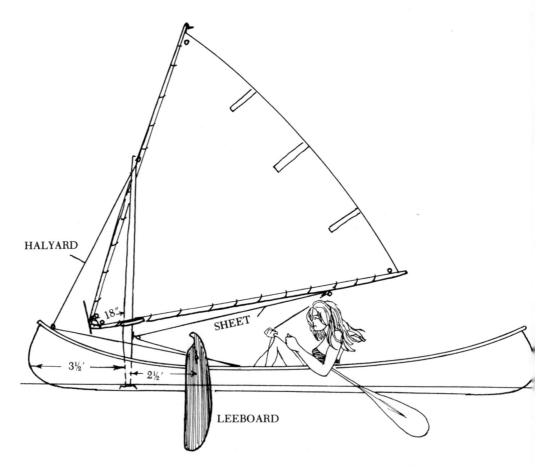

Rigging the canoe.

per and the regular cleat. The sheet is fastened around the center thwart and proceeds forward through the block near the base of the mast, aft to the block on the boom, and finally to the skipper and the jam cleat.

Sailing the rig in a variety of situations and conditions is the only way to get a real feeling for it and to determine the optimum position of all parts and rigging. The builder should not hesitate to alter the rig in any manner that will increase performance or make the canoe easier for him to handle. The option of converting the canoe to a miniature sailing yacht is a handy one that will surely increase the overall enjoyment the owner/builder will derive from his canoe.

Appendix

Lumber Sources

Penberthy Lumber Company
5800 South Boyle Avenue
Los Angeles, California 90058
(213) 583-4511

   Ash, mahogany, maple, white oak, spruce.

Yukon Lumber Company
520 West 22nd Street
Norfolk, Virginia 23517
(804) 625-7131

   Honduras and Philippine mahogany, white oak, Sitka spruce, ash, white cedar;
   millwork.

Maurice L. Condon Company, Inc.
250 Ferris Avenue
White Plains, New York 10603
(914) 946-4111

   Sitka spruce, Honduras and Philippine mahogany, white oak, western red
   cedar, Virginia white cedar, Alaska yellow cedar; millwork.

F. Scott Jay and Company, Inc.
P.O. Box 146
8174 Ritchie Highway
Pasadena, Maryland 21122

   White oak, ash, Honduras and Philippine mahogany, Sitka spruce, western red
   cedar, maple, white cedar.

Kiever-Willard Lumber Company
11-13 Graf Road
Newbury, Massachusetts 01950
(617) 462-7193

   Sitka spruce, western red cedar, white oak, Honduras and Philippine
   mahogany.

AUTHOR'S NOTE: Again I will emphasize that the prospective builder should exhaust all local sources of lumber, no matter how small, before resorting to one of the above-listed dealers, who specialize in handling relatively large accounts.

Fastenings

William Alvarez and Company
P.O. Box 245
350 East Orangethorpe Avenue, Unit 5
Placentia, California 92670
(714) 993-2960

Bronze carriage bolts and machine screws, brass finishing washers, bronze wood screws, bronze threaded boat nails.

Majestic Fasteners, Inc.
P.O. Box 193
Morris Plains, New Jersey 07950
(201) 386-1616

Bronze carriage bolts, bronze and brass machine screws, brass finishing washers, brass and bronze wood screws, bronze threaded boat nails.

Old Town Canoe Company
35 Middle Street
Old Town, Maine 04468

Brass canoe tacks, brass bolts.

Island Falls Canoe Company
RFD #3 Box 76
Atkinson Mills
Dover-Foxcroft, Maine 04426

Brass canoe tacks.

Androscoggin Boat and Canoe Company
Wayne, Maine 04284
(207) 685-9925

Brass canoe tacks.

Freedom Boat Works
Route 1, Box 12
North Freedom, Wisconsin 53951
(608) 356-5861

Brass canoe tacks and brass bolts.

McGreivey's Canoe Shop
Victory Village
Cato, New York 13033
(315) 626-6635

Canoe tacks, nails, bolts.

Rollin Thurlow
Northwoods Canoe Shop
Kenduskeag, Maine 04456
(207) 884-7723

Canoe tacks, nails, bolts.

Standard Fastenings
2 Pequod Road
Fairhaven, Mass. 02719
(617) 993-1791

Nails, bolts.

Paints and Varnishes, Oils and Bedding Compounds

Kirby Paint Company
163 Mount Vernon Street
New Bedford, Massachusetts 02740
(617) 997-9008

Pettit Paint Company, Inc.
Rockaway, New Jersey 07866

Woolsey Marine Industries, Inc.
New York, New York

Andrew Brown Company, Inc.
Los Angeles, California
Seattle, Washington
Irving, Texas
Laurel, Maryland

Interlux Paint Company, Inc.
New York, New York 10004

AUTHOR'S NOTE: Write for name of local distributor and list of products.

Canvas Filler

Old Town Canoe Company
35 Middle Street
Old Town, Maine 04468

Rollin Thurlow
Northwoods Canoe Shop
Kenduskeag, Maine 04456
(207) 884-7723

McGreivey's Canoe Shop
Victory Village
Cato, New York 13033
(315) 626-6635

Island Falls Canoe Company
RFD #3 Box 76
Atkinson Mills
Dover-Foxcroft, Maine 04426

AUTHOR'S NOTE: Check paint manufacturers for alternate filling/water-proofing systems for canvas other than the one detailed in the text.

Canvas

Harry Miller Company, Inc.
540 E Street
Boston, Massachusetts 02210
(617) 423-0300

McGreivey's Canoe Shop
Victory Village
Cato, New York 13033
(315) 626-6635

Rollin Thurlow
Northwoods Canoe Shop
Kenduskeag, Maine 04456
(207) 884-7723

Sailmakers

Hale's Sail Loft
Sargentville, Maine 04673
(207) 395-8913

Nathaniel Wilson, Sailmaker
Box 71
East Boothbay, Maine 04544
(207) 633-5071

Glenn Housley, Sailmakers
616 Third Street
Annapolis, Maryland 21403
(301) 263-4913

Yardarm Sailmakers
925 Webster Street
Needham, Massachusetts 02192
(617) 444-7060

Johnson & Joseph Company
1155 Embarcadero
Oakland, California 94606
(415) 832-5420

Woodworking and Special Tools

Garrett Wade Company, Inc.
302 Fifth Avenue
New York, New York 10001

Brookstone Company
5 Vose Farm Road
Peterborough, New Hampshire 03458

Woodcraft Supply Corporation
313 Montvale Avenue
Woburn, Massachusetts 01801

The Wooden Boat Shop
1007 Northeast Boat Street
Seattle, Washington 98105
(206) 634-3600

The Toolroom
East Oxbow Road
Shelburne Falls, Massachusetts 01370

Seat Cane

The H.H. Perkins Company
10 South Bradley Road
Woodbridge, Connecticut 06525

   Natural cane and cane fillers.

Frank's Cane and Rush Supply
7244 Heil Avenue
Huntington Beach, California 92647

Sources of Plans

Plans and offsets, templates, and complete kits for building a 17'5" guide canoe
very similar to the 18'6" canoe described in the text are available from Rollin
Thurlow, Northwoods Canoe Shop, Kenduskeag, Maine 04456.

Books that supply plans for canoes of different construction but adaptable to
wood-canvas include:

Atwood Manley, *Rushton and His Times in American Canoeing*, Syracuse
   University Press, Syracuse, New York, 1968.

David Hazen, *The Stripper's Guide to Canoe-building*, third ed., Tamal Vista
   Publications, San Francisco, California, 1976.

Gil Gilpatrick, *Building a Strip Canoe*, DeLorme Publishing Co., P.O. Box 87,
   Yarmouth, Maine 04096, 1979.

Index

254

Edge-set, 131
Eyebolts, 246, 247

Fairing block, 64-65, 115-117
Fairing procedures, 27-29
Fastenings, 46-48; for gunwales, 148, 202; for half-ribs, 160; for mast step, 246; for planking, 127-129, 148-150; for sheathing, 29; for spars, 245-246; for strong-back, 31-32
Fiberglass canoes, 14
Fiberglass cloth covering, 5, 10, 12, 167
Fillers, canvas, 49, 227; application of, 178, 184-190; curing of, 191
Fishing canoes, 10, 14
Forms, canoe, 22
Frames. *See* Ribs

Gaff, 245
Garboard, 126, 127-129
Gasoline-powered canoes, 18
Glues, waterproof, 197
Grand Lake chain, 17
Grand Lake Matagamon, 8
Grand Lake Stream, 17
Grand Lake Stream canoe, 17-18
Gray, George, 14
Greenville, ME, 8, 10
Guide canoes, 4, 9, 11, 17, 18
Gunwale backers, 29-31
Gunwales: fastenings for, 46; installation of, 144-148, 201-202; preparation of, 61-62, 73-77, 94-98; replacement of, 223; woods used for, 42-45

Half-ribs, 112, 157-160
Halyard, 246, 247
Hardwoods, 42, 44

Indian canoes, 1-3
Inwales, 14, 74, 77, 222
Island Falls Canoe Company, 18-19

Jigs: construction of, 61-62; use of, 94-104

Kayaks, 14
Keels: construction of, 202-205;

fastenings for, 46; repair of, 227; woods used for, 46
Kennebec canoes, 4
Kennebec River, 8

Lapstrake canoes, 4
Lateen rig, 242, 245
Lavoie, Joe, 14
Leeboards, 247
Levenseller, Boot, 14
Linseed oil, 214, 232
Lubec, ME, 18

Machias River, 17
Mahogany, 18, 44, 213
Maine, canoe building in, 4-19
Mast, 244
Mast step, 245, 246
Milling of stock, 72-91
Milo, ME, 11
Molds, canoe, 22-25, 32
Moore, Laurence ("Pop"), 17, 18
Moosehead Lake, 8
Moose River, 8
Morris canoes, 4
Mortise-and-tenon joints, 144, 195
Mt. Kineo, 8

Nails, ring, 46
Nomad sailing canoe, 18
North East Carry, 8

Oak, 45, 46
Old Town Canoe Company, 4, 14-16
Old Town, ME, 14
Outboard motors, 17

Paddle making, 12, 230-232
Paddling positions, 194
Paints: enamel, 214-215; epoxy, 215
Penobscot River, 8
Pine, 25, 42
Plan, body, 24
Planking: pattern, 124-126; preparation of, 77-81; repair of, 223; woods used for, 15-16, 18, 42
Plastic canoes, 4, 5, 14
Poles, 232-239
Polyurethane, 29, 212, 232
Prebending, 94-98